Workshop on NLG for Human-Robot Interaction 2018

Tilburg, The Netherlands
8 November 2018

ISBN: 978-1-5108-7755-9

Printed from e-media with permission by:

Curran Associates, Inc.
57 Morehouse Lane
Red Hook, NY 12571

Some format issues inherent in the e-media version may also appear in this print version.

Printed by Curran Associates, Inc. (2019)

For permission requests, please contact the Association for Computational Linguistics at the address below.

Association for Computational Linguistics
209 N. Eighth Street
Stroudsburg, Pennsylvania 18360

Phone: 1-570-476-8006
Fax: 1-570-476-0860

acl@aclweb.org

Additional copies of this publication are available from:

Curran Associates, Inc.
57 Morehouse Lane
Red Hook, NY 12571 USA
Phone: 845-758-0400
Fax: 845-758-2633
Email: curran@proceedings.com
Web: www.proceedings.com

INLG 2018

Workshop on
NLG for Human–Robot Interaction

Proceedings of the Workshop

November 8, 2018
Tilburg, The Netherlands

Workshop on NLG for Human–Robot Interaction
November 8, 2018, Tilburg, The Netherlands
http://purl.org/net/nlg-hri-workshop-2018/

Download this proceedings from: http://aclweb.org/anthology/W18-69

Order copies of this and other ACL proceedings from:

Association for Computational Linguistics (ACL)
209 N. Eighth Street
Stroudsburg, PA 18360
USA
Tel: +1-570-476-8006
Fax: +1-570-476-0860
acl@aclweb.org

Introduction

The workshop on NLG for Human–Robot Interaction (NLG-HRI) was held in Tilburg, The Netherlands as part of the 11th International Conference on Natural Language Generation (INLG 2018).

The aim of the workshop was to bring the two research communities Natural Language Generation (NLG) and Human–Robot Interaction (HRI) together in order to enable an interdisciplinary dialogue between researchers of these fields.

The workshop invited short position papers from researchers working on human–robot interaction and/or natural language generation. The workshop received eight submissions, all of which were reviewed by two or three members of the program committee. Five of papers were chosen for long oral presentations (15 minutes), and three for short oral presentations (7 minutes). This proceedings volume contains the six papers whose authors agreed to have their position papers published.

The workshop began with a short tutorial-style introductions to the fields involved. This was followed by presentations of the position papers. In the afternoon, two break-out groups were formed for in-depth discussion of (i) interactive multimodal generation, and (ii) shared tasks, challenges, and tools. Finally, future actions on the topics of the workshop as well as ways to continue the conversation were discussed.

Thirty-two participants registered for the workshop, most of them working on natural language generation, some on natural language generation for human–robot interaction (or interactive systems more generally) and a few on human–robot interaction. Attendees engaged in lively discussions around the presented papers and the topics of the break-out groups, making the workshop a success.

We would, once again, like to thank the authors, the program committee members, and the workshop attendees.

Mary Ellen Foster
Hendrik Buschmeier
Dimitra Gkatzia

Organizers:

Mary Ellen Foster, University of Glasgow
Hendrik Buschmeier, Bielefeld University
Dimitra Gkatzia, Edinburgh Napier University

Program Committee:

Elisabeth André, University of Augsburg (Germany)
Joyce Chai, Michigan State University (USA)
Manuel Giuliani, UWE Bristol (UK)
Julian Hough, Queen Mary University of London (UK)
Amy Isard, University of Edinburgh (UK)
Kristiina Jokinen, AI Research Center, AIST Tokyo Waterfront (Japan)
Stefan Kopp, Bielefeld University (Germany)
Emiel Krahmer, Tilburg University (The Netherlands)
Matthew Purver, Queen Mary University of London (UK)
David Schlangen, Bielefeld University (Germany)
Kristina Striegnitz, Union College (USA)
Mariët Theune, University of Twente (The Netherlands)
Graham Wilcock, CDM Interact, Helsinki (Finland)

Table of Contents

Context-sensitive Natural Language Generation for robot-assisted second language tutoring
Bram Willemsen, Jan de Wit, Emiel Krahmer, Mirjam de Haas and Paul Vogt 1

Learning from limited datasets: Implications for Natural Language Generation and Human-Robot Interaction
Jekaterina Belakova and Dimitra Gkatzia 8

Shaping a social robot's humor with Natural Language Generation and socially-aware reinforcement learning
Hannes Ritschel and Elisabeth André 12

From sensors to sense: Integrated heterogeneous ontologies for Natural Language Generation
Mihai Pomarlan, Robert Porzel, John Bateman and Rainer Malaka 17

A farewell to arms: Non-verbal communication for non-humanoid robots
Aaron G. Cass, Kristina Striegnitz and Nick Webb 22

Being data-driven is not enough: Revisiting interactive instruction giving as a challenge for NLG
Sina Zarrieß and David Schlangen 27

Conference Program

Thursday, November 8, 2018

9:00–10:30 Introduction

9:00–9:10 Welcome

9:10–10:10 *Introduction to NLG for HRI by Mary Ellen Foster*

10:10–10:30 *Discussion*

10:30–11:00 Coffee break

11:00–12:30 Presentation Session 1

11:00–11:20 *Context-sensitive Natural Language Generation for robot-assisted second language tutoring*
Bram Willemsen, Jan de Wit, Emiel Krahmer, Mirjam de Haas and Paul Vogt

11:20–11:30 *Learning from limited datasets: Implications for Natural Language Generation and Human-Robot Interaction*
Jekaterina Belakova and Dimitra Gkatzia

11:30–11:40 *A NLG based error reporting system for production line machines*
Frank Feulner, Robert Weißgraeber, Alexander Deutsch and Stefan Lasse

11:40–11:50 *Building a large-scale Persona dialog dataset*
Yinhe Zheng, Guanyi Chen and Minlie Huang

11:50–12:10 *Shaping a social robot's humor with Natural Language Generation and socially-aware reinforcement learning*
Hannes Ritschel and Elisabeth André

12:10–12:30 *From sensors to sense: Integrated heterogeneous ontologies for Natural Language Generation*
Mihai Pomarlan, Robert Porzel, John Bateman and Rainer Malaka

12:30–13:30 Lunch

Thursday, November 8, 2018 (continued)

13:30–14:10 Presentation Session 2

13:30–13:50 *A farewell to arms: Non-verbal communication for non-humanoid robots*
Aaron G. Cass, Kristina Striegnitz and Nick Webb

13:50–14:10 *Being data-driven is not enough: Revisiting interactive instruction giving as a challenge for NLG*
Sina Zarrieß and David Schlangen

14:10–16:30 Break-out groups

14:10–14:20 *Organisation*

14:20–15:00 *Break-out groups*

15:00–15:30 Coffee break

15:30–16:10 *Break-out groups (cont')*

16:10–16:30 *Results*

16:30–17:00 Wrap-up

16:30–16:55 *Discussion of future actions*

16:55–17:00 Farewell

Context-Sensitive Natural Language Generation for Robot-Assisted Second Language Tutoring

Bram Willemsen, Jan de Wit, Emiel Krahmer, Mirjam de Haas, Paul Vogt
Tilburg School of Humanities and Digital Sciences, Tilburg University, The Netherlands
{b.willemsen,j.m.s.dewit,e.j.krahmer,mirjam.dehaas,p.a.vogt}@uvt.nl

Abstract

This paper describes the L2TOR intelligent tutoring system (ITS), focusing primarily on its output generation module. The L2TOR ITS is developed for the purpose of investigating the efficacy of robot-assisted second language tutoring in early childhood. We explain the process of generating contextually-relevant utterances, such as task-specific feedback messages, and discuss challenges regarding multimodality and multilingualism for situated natural language generation from a robot tutoring perspective.

1 Introduction

In recent years, an increasing body of work has highlighted the potential of social robots for various educational purposes (Mubin et al., 2013; Belpaeme et al., 2018a). This paper describes research conducted in the context of second language (L2) acquisition in early childhood as part of a project called Second Language Tutoring using Social Robots, or **L2TOR** for short (Belpaeme et al., 2015). The main goal of the L2TOR project is to evaluate the possible benefits of using social robots as (second) language tutors; more specifically, the aim is to provide tentative guidelines to aid the development and deployment of robot-assisted platforms suitable to teach children between the ages of five and six an L2 (Belpaeme et al., 2015, 2018b).

The rationale behind the use of a social robot for the purpose of L2 tutoring is multifold. A noted benefit is the possibility of providing more one-to-one tutoring (Belpaeme et al., 2018a). An advantage of the embodied aspect of a robot tutor is its social and physical presence in the referential world of the learner (Leyzberg et al., 2012). A humanoid robot may capitalise on its anthropomorphic appearance by non-verbally communicating with the learner, such as through the use of gestures, a scaffolding mechanism which has been shown to have positive effects on learning outcomes when used by human tutors (e.g., Hald et al., 2016; Alibali and Nathan, 2007; Tellier, 2008) and may similarly benefit children learning an L2 from a robot tutor (de Wit et al., 2018).

An important aspect in the development of the L2TOR system is the human element; findings from studies of human tutors are leading in the design of the robot's behaviours. The aforementioned use of gestures is an example of non-verbal behaviours to be incorporated into the tutoring interactions. With respect to the verbal behaviours of the robot, the aim is to tailor the lexical output to the situational context of the learner when appropriate. To this end, we turn to natural language generation (NLG). Through context-sensitive NLG, we will be able to provide, among other things, situationally-relevant feedback messages. Adjusting output to fit the situational context is expected to make interactions between child and robot more natural. Situated NLG for human-robot interaction (HRI), however, is a rather complex matter which requires us to address various issues not typically of concern to more conventional applications of NLG. We will discuss in more detail the design choices and challenges encountered with respect to the development of the L2TOR system's multimodal and multilingual output generation module.

2 L2TOR ITS

The L2TOR system is designed to be a state-of-the-art robot-assisted intelligent tutoring sys-

Proceedings of the Workshop on NLG for Human–Robot Interaction, pages 1–7,
Tilburg, The Netherlands, November 8, 2018. © 2018 Association for Computational Linguistics

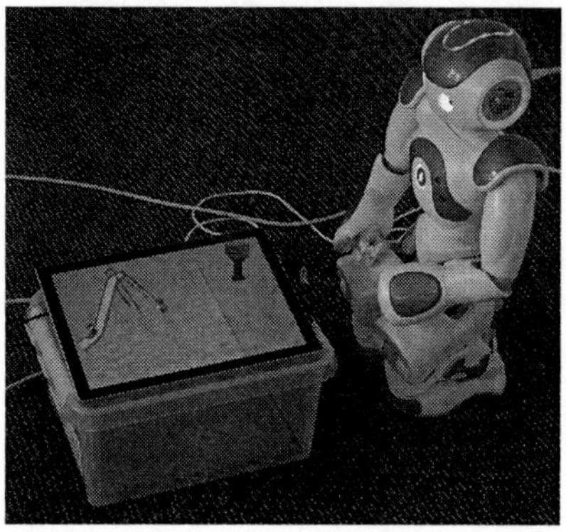

Figure 1: The basic setup of the L2TOR ITS.

tem (ITS) intended to teach young children an L2. The hardware components that constitute the system's learning environment are SoftBank Robotic's NAO humanoid robot and a tablet computer. The basic setup is shown in Figure 1. Combined with promising technologies, such as knowledge tracing (Schodde et al., 2017; de Wit et al., 2018), the motivation behind the system's design is to facilitate the transfer of pedagogical techniques used by human tutors to the robot tutoring domain.

The architecture of the L2TOR ITS is modular in nature; modules in the system are each responsible for dealing with specific parts of the tutoring interaction, including the registration and interpretation of learner inputs, the management of interaction flow and the relaying of relevant information to other parts of the system, and the generation of appropriate behaviours on the basis of knowledge representations derived from learner inputs and situational context. It should be noted that the system relies on the tablet computer to mediate interactions, as automatic speech recognition was considered insufficiently reliable to serve as an input device for child-robot interactions (Kennedy et al., 2017; Belpaeme et al., 2018b).

With the intention of investigating the efficacy of robot-assisted L2 vocabulary training in a longitudinal setting (Belpaeme et al., 2015, 2018b), a series of lessons was developed in conjunction with the L2TOR ITS. The curriculum covered two educational domains, namely the number domain, which involves number words and (pre-)mathematical concepts, and the space domain, which covers basic spatial relations. A total of 34 target words were selected based on a systematic review of educational curricula and standard literacy tests. The lessons were designed to cover, on average, six of the target words per tutoring session. Children were to interact with the robot on seven occasions, i.e., six lessons covering both educational domains followed by a recap session, over the course of roughly three weeks.

3 Generating Output

In the L2TOR ITS, the module responsible for realizing any and all robot output is referred to as the *Output Module*. This output includes both verbal and non-verbal behaviours. Verbal behaviours are realised as synthesised speech through a text-to-speech (TTS) engine. Verbal output is combined with the appropriate non-verbal behaviours such as (co-speech) gestures as well as gaze, all of which is coordinated with accompanying actions on the tablet computer. The Output Module comprises several submodules, each responsible for their own part in the planning and realization of the robot's behaviours. One of these submodules is concerned with the generation of contextually-relevant feedback messages.

The primary purpose of situated NLG for HRI is the contextualisation of output. For a tutoring interaction this means that we would want NLG to be able to take into account the current state of affairs regarding the subject matter as well as the learner's inputs at any point in the interaction to provide them with adequate information, including feedback. In addition, NLG might help make interactions more dynamic by adding variation. Note, however, that certain components, including NLG, in the iteration of the ITS intended to be evaluated in a longitudinal study (Belpaeme et al., 2015, 2018b) are more constrained for reasons of experimental consistency; applications of the system outside of research would ideally increase the level of adaptation and personalization.

3.1 Curriculum

The content of the lessons was designed to provide meaningful context to the target words; in the virtual environment presented on the tablet computer, the children would visit several locations and take part in activities that were related to the language input the child received and which were expected to speak to their imagination. For example, together with the robot, the child would visit the zoo and interact with the animals to learn about numbers and (pre-)mathematical concepts. Activities

```
"objective": {
    "id": "cage",
    "is_plural": false,
    "rel": {
        "target": {
            "id": "animal",
            "is_plural": true
        },
    "type": "most"
    }
}
```

Figure 2: JSON-formatted data structure containing information regarding current state of the interaction.

```
"monkey": {
    "Dutch": {
        "plural": {
            "article": "de",
            "text": "apen"
        },
        "singular": {
            "article": "de",
            "text": "aap"
        }
    }
}
```

Figure 3: Sample of dictionary containing information on various task-related words and phrases.

then took the form of various tasks. With the tablet in use as the main input device, most of these activities concerned interactions with objects shown on screen (e.g., selecting and moving objects).

The lesson content is stored in so-called *storyboards*. These storyboards are essentially annotated scripts in the form of spreadsheets. They contain line-by-line information regarding expected robot and tablet output at any point in the interaction. Although these storyboards can be amended by non-experts, they are not stored in a machine-readable format. We, therefore, use a custom parser to transform them to a JSON-like format such as shown in Figure 2.

3.2 State Tracking

Even though it is possible to generate contextually-relevant feedback and task descriptions to a certain extent when only the task type and the objects involved are known, this no longer holds when the context requires us to distinguish between several (seemingly) identical objects in order to generate the correct referring expression. For example, this is problematic when a task requires the learner to touch, in the virtual environment on screen, the cage *containing most animals*, but multiple cages are shown. The system will only know that the object associated with task completion is a cage with a specific identifier (ID); this ID is not mapped to any representation that uniquely identifies the object from the others in natural language.

To ensure that the system is aware of which object, in our example *which cage*, was the correct answer, while also being able to generate a description that uniquely identifies it, we implemented a discourse model to keep track of the system's current state — in this case the positions of all virtual objects on the tablet — over the course of the interaction. To make sure that these object descriptions are generalizable to different languages and various situations, the model stores data structures, such as shown in Figure 2, instead of full utterances. The components of this data structure (cage, containing, most, animals) can then be translated using a dictionary, such as shown in Figure 3, before being inserted into the correct syntactic template. The conversion between object IDs and their descriptions is currently performed offline, i.e., prior to the interaction rather than during, when parsing the storyboards. During the interaction, the discourse model is supplemented by functionalities from Underworlds (Lemaignan et al., 2018), a spatial and temporal modelling framework, which tracks, in real time, whether certain tasks have been correctly carried out in the virtual environment.

3.3 NLG

As a result of the task-driven and scripted nature of the tutoring interactions, NLG serves a niche purpose within the ITS. Although progress has been made with respect to end-to-end NLG systems (Gatt and Krahmer, 2018), given the focused domain of application, namely situated NLG for robot-assisted L2 acquisition, we have instead opted for a template-based approach (van Deemter et al., 2003; Gatt and Krahmer, 2018) as this allows us to exert the necessary control over the output, both verbal and non-verbal, to ensure its quality. Similarly to other data-to-text systems (Gatt and Krahmer, 2018), we use hand-crafted syntactic templates and fill gaps with task-specific information. This information is derived from data structures such as shown in Figure 2 and Figure 3.

Part of the interaction for which NLG is re-

"Nee, dat klopt niet helemaal. [No, that's not quite right.]
Je moet **the monkey** in de kooi *aanraken.* [You need to touch **the monkey** in the cage.]
Probeer het nog maar een keer." [Try again.]

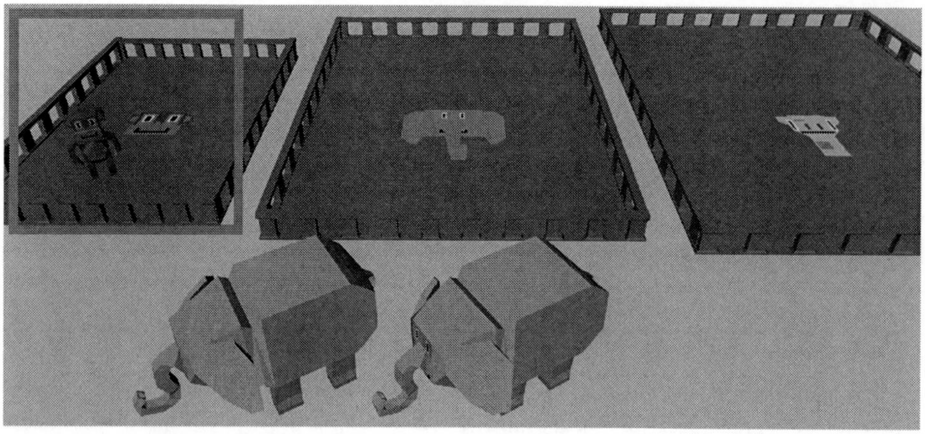

Figure 4: Example of an object selection task presented on the tablet computer. For this hypothetical scenario we assume the L1 to be Dutch and the L2 to be English. The learner was asked to touch the monkey in the cage — here shown in the (pink) box —, but has instead touched one of the elephants shown in the foreground. The robot will now provide the feedback message as shown above the image (in italics). Note that neither the (pink) box nor the text are visible to the learner.

quired is the contextualisation of feedback. Rather than telling the learner their execution of a task was either wrong or right, we want to be able to comment on the exact nature of their actions in relation to what was required of them for task completion. The information required to make feedback messages contextually relevant varies per task, as does the way in which this information is organised. For this reason, different tasks require the use of different syntactic templates for the provision of adequate feedback.

To illustrate the process of constructing a contextually-relevant feedback message, Figure 4 provides an example of an incorrectly-executed object selection task in an interaction in which the L1 is Dutch. At this point in the interaction, there are several animals shown on screen, one of which is shown inside an enclosure (referred to as cage), namely the monkey; two elephants, however, have managed to escape. The learner is asked to touch the monkey residing inside the cage, but does not manage to do so. In order to provide feedback to the learner, we use the template as shown in Table 1. The template contains a preposition (**$prep**) explaining the relationship between two objects, here labeled as **$trg** (target) and **$obj** (object). In our example, the target is the noun phrase *the monkey* and the object is the noun phrase *the cage* (*de kooi* in Dutch). In order to retrieve the correct form, we consult a dictionary with information regarding the objects in question, such as shown in Figure 3. If the target in our example had been addressed in the L1, we would have retrieved the Dutch singular version of the noun phrase, i.e., the determiner *de* [the] and the noun *aap* [monkey]. To complete the feedback message, the syntactic template is preceded by a feedback phrase indicating more explicitly that an incorrect answer was provided, and followed by a prompt telling the learner to attempt the task once more. Although the prompt is hard-coded, the feedback phrase concerns a random selection, without immediate repetition, from a set of canned expressions as a way of introducing some more variation to the message.

In addition, in the event that user input is not registered for an extended period of time, we attempt to re-engage the learner through a contextually-relevant prompt. This prompt is constructed in a similar manner as the feedback message, i.e., by means of slot-filling a task-relevant syntactic template, to remind the user of the current task.

3.4 Non-Verbal Behaviour

Human tutors often use gestures as a scaffolding mechanism (e.g., Alibali and Nathan, 2007).

(A)	Nee, dat klopt niet helemaal.	[No, that's not quite right.]
(B)	Je moet **$trg $prep $obj** aanraken.	[You need to touch **$trg $prep $obj**.]
(C)	Probeer het nog maar een keer.	[Try again.]

Table 1: Example of a feedback message for an object selection task. The message consists of three parts: (A) a (negative) feedback phrase, (B) the syntactic template, and (C) a prompt.

Thanks to the NAO's humanoid appearance, we can incorporate gestures into tutoring interactions in a similar manner. For gestures that coincide with speech, i.e., co-speech gestures, the proper alignment of speech and gesture is crucial. This behavioural management is a built-in functionality of the NAOqi API. The ALAnimatedSpeech module[1] processes text annotated with specific commands in order to tell the robot at which point in an utterance a behaviour, such as an iconic gesture, is to be executed. To improve the timing of the execution, we inserted timed pauses to synchronise the stroke of the gesture with the target word. Despite increased synchronisation, the added pauses do slow down the interaction.

In addition to iconic gestures, we make use of deictic gestures to guide the learner's attention. The combination of gaze and pointing gestures helps establish joint attention, while gaze may also help build rapport between child and robot (Admoni and Scassellati, 2017). All non-verbal behaviours are triggered from the annotated utterance, of which an example is shown in Table 2.

3.5 Speech Synthesis

In contrast with typical NLG applications, the surface realization of NLG for HRI is not a human-readable text, but instead a rendition of an utterance as synthesised speech. Depending on the language of choice, the TTS engine of the NAO robot is by default either powered by Nuance or Acapela. These TTS engines are both capable of producing a speech signal from a text string.

In the context of language acquisition, the quality of the synthesised speech may be of importance, as (young) learners have been shown to attend to non-verbal cues present in the speech signal when presented with a novel language (e.g., Dominey and Dodane, 2004). Although the effects of speech synthesis quality on learners' perceptions have previously been studied for computer-assisted language learning (e.g., Bione et al., 2016; Handley, 2009; Kang et al., 2008), whether poor quality speech synthesis impedes the efficacy of language acquisition has not been unequivocally established.

Although both the Nuance and Acapela TTS engines allow for modification of the speech signal to a certain extent by means of parameter tuning (e.g., pitch, volume, speaking rate), control over the quality of the synthesised speech is limited. The multilingual nature of the interaction causes additional difficulties, as code-switching in the current iteration of the ITS requires us to switch TTS engine frequently, often within the same utterance. As a result of the engines only receiving segments of the utterance rather than the utterance as a whole, the quality of the speech signal is negatively affected as words and phrases, in particular near segmentation boundaries, are mispronounced to varying degrees. It should be noted that the switch of engine also results in a change of voice, as different languages have been dictated by different speakers.

Despite certain difficulties being inherent to the technologies themselves, we have managed to address some of the TTS problems we have encountered. For example, in order to correct some of the pronunciation errors, we have relied on phonetic transcriptions of problematic words and phrases. Take, for instance, the word *tablet*. When the L1 is Dutch, the TTS will pronounce the word as the Dutch word for *pill*, rather than the intended pronunciation referring to a tablet computer. However, when we use the following phonetic representation of the word: `t E: b l @ t`, the synthesised speech will more closely resemble the expected pronunciation. Furthermore, to avoid any chance of poorly synthesised speech being a learner's first exposure to a target word in the L2, we instead make use of audio recordings of a native speaker, played back via the tablet's speakers.

4 Conclusion

In this paper, we have described the L2TOR ITS, focussing primarily on the system's multimodal

[1]http://doc.aldebaran.com/2-1/naoqi/audio/alanimatedspeech.html

Kijk **John** `^start(pointing/tablet)` `$toggle_facetracking=False` `^start(gaze/tablet)`,
de dieren spelen een spelletje met ons! `$toggle_facetracking=True`

[Look **John** `^start(pointing/tablet)` `$toggle_facetracking=False` `^start(gaze/tablet)`,
the animals are playing a game with us! `$toggle_facetracking=True`]

Table 2: Example of an annotated utterance returned by the Output Module. Here, **John** is the child's given name. **^start(pointing/tablet)** indicates that the robot will direct the attention of the child to the tablet by using a pointing gesture. As can be seen from **$toggle_facetracking=False**, face tracking is then disabled, after which the robot will direct its own gaze towards the tablet, **^start(gaze/tablet)**, in an attempt to establish joint attention. At the end of the utterance, face tracking is once again enabled.

and multilingual output generation module. We have discussed challenges with respect to situated NLG for the purpose of robot-assisted language tutoring, including natural-sounding TTS, multimodality and multilingualism, coordinating robot actions and tablet output, and how and to what extent these were addressed within the context of the project.

Acknowledgements

This work is funded by Horizon 2020, the EU Framework Programme for Research and Innovation, Grant Agreement: 688014, and the Tilburg School of Humanities and Digital Sciences at Tilburg University, The Netherlands.

References

Henny Admoni and Brian Scassellati. 2017. Social Eye Gaze in Human-Robot Interaction: A Review. *Journal of Human-Robot Interaction*, 6(1):25–63.

Martha W Alibali and Mitchell J Nathan. 2007. Teachers' Gestures as a Means of Scaffolding Students' Understanding: Evidence From an Early Algebra Lesson. *Video Research in the Learning Sciences*, 39(5):349–366.

Tony Belpaeme, James Kennedy, Paul Baxter, Paul Vogt, Emiel E J Krahmer, Stefan Kopp, Kirsten Bergmann, Paul Leseman, Aylin C Küntay, Tilbe Göksun, Amit K Pandey, Rodolphe Gelin, Petra Koudelkova, and Tommy Deblieck. 2015. L2TOR - Second Language Tutoring using Social Robots. In *Proceedings of the First International Workshop on Educational Robotics at ICSR 2015*.

Tony Belpaeme, James Kennedy, Aditi Ramachandran, Brian Scassellati, and Fumihide Tanaka. 2018a. Social robots for education: A review. *Science Robotics*, 3(21):eaat5954.

Tony Belpaeme, Paul Vogt, Rianne van den Berghe, Kirsten Bergmann, Tilbe Göksun, Mirjam de Haas, Junko Kanero, James Kennedy, Aylin C. Küntay, Ora Oudgenoeg-Paz, Fotios Papadopoulos, Thorsten Schodde, Josje Verhagen, Christopher D. Wallbridge, Bram Willemsen, Jan de Wit, Vasfiye Geçkin, Laura Hoffmann, Stefan Kopp, Emiel Krahmer, Ezgi Mamus, Jean Marc Montanier, Cansu Oranç, and Amit Kumar Pandey. 2018b. Guidelines for Designing Social Robots as Second Language Tutors. *International Journal of Social Robotics*, 10(3):325–341.

Tiago Bione, Jennica Grimshaw, and Walcir Cardoso. 2016. An evaluation of text-to-speech synthesizers in the foreign language classroom: learners' perceptions. In *CALL communities and culture short papers from EUROCALL 2016*, pages 50–54.

Kees van Deemter, Mariët Theune, and Emiel Krahmer. 2003. Real vs. template-based natural language generation: a false opposition? *Computational Linguistics*, 31:15–24.

Peter F. Dominey and Christelle Dodane. 2004. Indeterminacy in language acquisition: the role of child directed speech and joint attention. *Journal of Neurolinguistics*, 17(2-3):121–145.

Albert Gatt and Emiel Krahmer. 2018. Survey of the State of the Art in Natural Language Generation: Core tasks, applications and evaluation. *Journal of Artificial Intelligence Research*, 61:65–170.

Lea A. Hald, Jacqueline de Nooijer, Tamara van Gog, and Harold Bekkering. 2016. Optimizing Word Learning via Links to Perceptual and Motoric Experience. *Educational Psychology Review*, 28(3):495–522.

Zöe Handley. 2009. Is text-to-speech synthesis ready for use in computer-assisted language learning? *Speech Communication*, 51(10):906–919.

Min Kang, Harumi Kashiwagi, Jutta Treviranus, and Makoto Kaburagi. 2008. Synthetic speech in foreign language learning: an evaluation by learners. *International Journal of Speech Technology*, 11(2):97–106.

James Kennedy, Severin Lemaignan, Caroline Montassier, Pauline Lavalade, Bahar Irfan, Fotios Papadopoulos, Emmanuel Senft, and Tony Belpaeme.

2017. Child Speech Recognition in Human-Robot Interaction: Evaluations and Recommendations. In *Proceedings of the 2017 ACM/IEEE International Conference on Human-Robot Interaction*, pages 82–90.

Séverin Lemaignan, Yoan Sallami, Christopher Wallbridge, Aurélie Clodic, Tony Belpaeme, and Rachid Alami. 2018. underworlds: Cascading Situation Assessment for Robots. In *Proceedings of the 2018 IEEE/RSJ International Conference on Intelligent Robots and Systems*.

Daniel Leyzberg, Samuel Spaulding, Mariya Toneva, and Brian Scassellati. 2012. The Physical Presence of a Robot Tutor Increases Cognitive Learning Gains. In *Proceedings of the 34th Annual Conference of the Cognitive Science Society*, pages 1882–1887.

Omar Mubin, Catherine J. Stevens, Suleman Shahid, Abdullah Al Mahmud, and Jian-Jie Dong. 2013. A Review of the Applicability of Robots in Education. *Technology for Education and Learning*, 1(1):1–7.

Thorsten Schodde, Kirsten Bergmann, and Stefan Kopp. 2017. Adaptive Robot Language Tutoring Based on Bayesian Knowledge Tracing and Predictive Decision-Making. In *Proceedings of the 2017 ACM/IEEE International Conference on Human-Robot Interaction*, pages 128–136.

Marion Tellier. 2008. The effect of gestures on second language memorisation by young children. *Gesture*, 8(2):219–235.

Jan de Wit, Thorsten Schodde, Bram Willemsen, Kirsten Bergmann, Mirjam de Haas, Stefan Kopp, Emiel Krahmer, and Paul Vogt. 2018. The Effect of a Robot's Gestures and Adaptive Tutoring on Children's Acquisition of Second Language Vocabularies. In *Proceedings of the 2018 ACM/IEEE International Conference on Human-Robot Interaction*, pages 50–58.

Learning from Limited Datasets: Implications for Natural Language Generation and Human-Robot Interaction

Jekaterina Belakova*
Kungshamra 71
Solna, 170 70
Sweden
ekaterinabeljakova@gmail.com

Dimitra Gkatzia
10 Colinton Road
Edinburgh, EH10 5DT
Edinburgh Napier University
d.gkatzia@napier.ac.uk

Abstract

One of the most natural ways for human robot communication is through spoken language. Training human-robot interaction systems require access to large datasets which are expensive to obtain and labour intensive. In this paper, we describe an approach for learning from minimal data, using as a toy example language understanding in spoken dialogue systems. Understanding of spoken language is crucial because it has implications for natural language generation, i.e. correctly understanding a user's utterance will lead to choosing the right response/action. Finally, we discuss implications for Natural Language Generation in Human-Robot Interaction.

1 Introduction

Robots are becoming prevalent as the technology advances and the prices drop. The International Federation of Robotics[1] reported that in 2017, there was a worldwide increase of 30% for industrial robots sales and there is a 39% increase of professional service robots the sales (in value), while forecasting a growth of 30-35% per year until 2020 for domestic robotics. This will create opportunities for effective human robot communication and will require robots to combine different skills such as computer vision, language understanding and generation as well as object manipulation.

Human-robot interaction (HRI) can be enhanced via the use of natural language dialogue between humans and robots. In this paper, we discuss the implications of dialogue for HRI, by deriving insights from recent work on personal assistants. In particular, we describe how `one-shot learning` can guide natural language generation in scenarios where we only have access to small amounts of example dialogues and discuss how we can transfer lessons learnt to human robot communication. Therefore, we initially describe the development of a personal assistant capable to handle users' queries without being trained with example dialogues, and then we describe how we can adapt this approach to human-robot communication.

2 Approach

MOOBO is a personal assistant for an educational platform Moodle[2] that takes as input users queries (such as queries regarding coursework, dealines, etc.) and outputs responses. Moodle is used by a large number of universities and it allows lectures to share their learning materials such as slides, academic papers, laboratory work as well as coursework and assignments. The students can then access all these documents and posts for their courses. This data becomes available in both a structured and unstructured way. MOOBO is able to access this data and extract the relevant information and render it to users in natural language.

2.1 Software Architecture

MOOBO is a web-based, platform independent application and available to use on all devices: desktops, tablets and mobiles. It uses a client-server architectural style which consists of two components, the client and the server, as shown in Figure 1. The client makes a call to the server and gets the response back. The server is contin-

*This work was completed while Jekaterina was a student at Edinburgh Napier University.

[1] https://ifr.org/

[2] https://moodle.org/

Proceedings of the Workshop on NLG for Human–Robot Interaction, pages 8–11,
Tilburg, The Netherlands, November 8, 2018.

uously listening to client requests. They communicate over HTTP using REST methods (such as GET, POST, PUT, DELETE) in a JSON format.

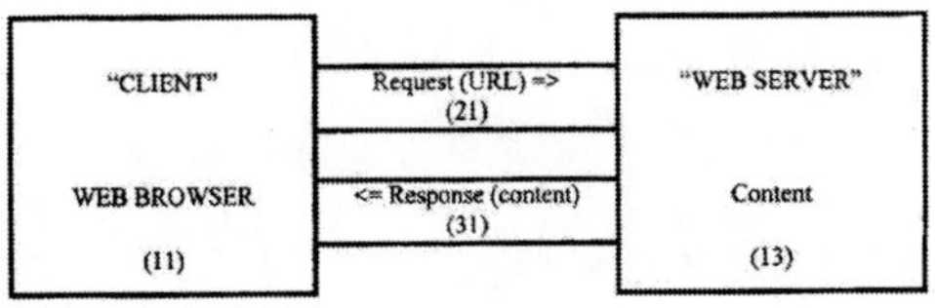

Figure 1: Client-server architecture

The client is a web browser passing on the user input to the server. It is developed using JavaScript framework, HTML and CSS. The server is developed in Python using Flask web framework that offers a development server and RESTful request dispatching.

MOOBO is effectively a spoken dialogue system and thus, it consists of five main components which are responsible for: Speech Recognition, Natural Language Understanding, Dialog Manager, Natural Language Generation and Text-to-Speech Synthesis as shown in Figure 2.

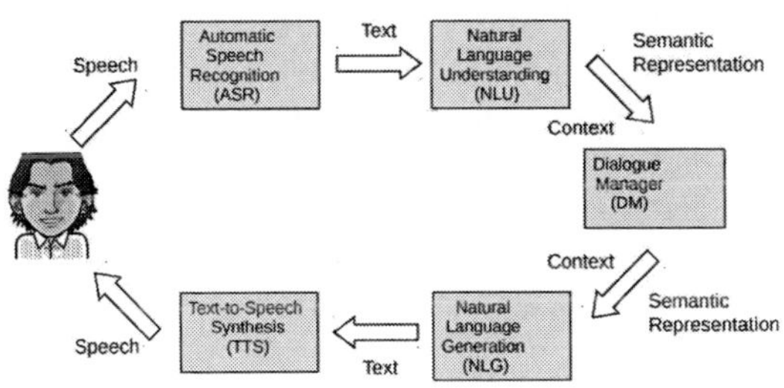

Figure 2: MOOBO's architecture.

Speech Recognition Speech Recognition uses a JavaScript library called `artyom.js` [3]. It resides on the client side and listens to the users input which is then forwarded to the server for further processing. To improve the user experience, both speech recognition and an option to write the input as a text are available.

Natural Language Understanding To process the user input, `spaCy` [4] was used in order to recognise Named Entities and part of speech.

Dialogue manager The Dialogue Manager (DM) is responsible for choosing the action which will lead to generating output. For this domain, dialogues were not available and therefore we created a small dataset of potential dialogues. Then each utterance was mapped to an intent as seen in Table 2. The main challenge that the dialogue manager needed to address is that different students ask for the same information in different ways. For instance, a student can ask "What is the module about?" and "What will I learn from the module?". Although these questions are phrased differently, the intent is the same: the student is requesting a module summary. When several examples of dialogues are available, it is easy to learn that both questions result in the same intent. However, when we only have one example of an intent, we need a clever way to associate all similar queries to this one example. Therefore, we used one-shot learning (Schroff et al., 2015) to address this challenge.

One-shot learning One-shot learning initially learns an embedding per instance usually using some deep learning approach. Once the embeddings have been produced, then the intend recognition simply becomes a k-NN classification problem. In our setup, one-shot learning was achieved as follows:

1. Utilising the knowledge of NER and part of speech tagging, embeddings of the natural language utterances were created using `Word2Vec` (Mikolov et al., 2013) with a 4-word window.

2. The K Nearest Neighbour algorithm (K-NN) was used to find the nearest utterance in the small dataset in terms of the Euclidean distance. After the Euclidean Distance is calculated, the system selects the three closest results and sorts them in terms of distance and selects the first one.

Because K-NN can be sensitive to outliers and has no confidence, the application used three nearest neighbours to make the result more stable.

There are six tasks that the system can perform as depicted in Table 2. They all require either information extraction or text summarization. This is different to traditional dialogue systems which utilise structured information stored in databases.

2.1.1 Natural Language Generation

After the DM has identified the right task, it sends it to the Natural Language Generation (NLG)

[3] https://sdkcarlos.github.io/sites/artyom.html
[4] https://spacy.io/

Input	Intent
What can I potentially learn from the module	module_summary
What is the coursework summary	cw_summary
What are my courses	course_summary
Who is the programme leader for the module	programme_leader
When is the coursework deadline	cw_deadline

Table 1: Examples of utterances mapped to intents.

Task Management
1. Coursework summary
2. Coursework deadline
3. Module summary
4. Course summary
5. Get a program leader
6. Lab/ Lecture summary

Table 2: List of MOOBO's actions.

module. At this instance, NLG is template-based with slot-filling.

Slot-filling in our project, required accessing unstructured text and deriving the correct information. Consider for instance the task of finding a program leader. The Named Entity Recognition module is used to look for a PERSON entity in a specific module section. The coursework deadline was extracted using Spacy NER DATE and ORGINAL types. Some coursework files were written in the specific template, which gave a possibility to use regular expressions to extract the information. For summaries generation TextRank was used (Mihalcea and Tarau, 2004). TextRank is a graph-based ranking algorithm which builds a graph, where the vertices are the units (extracted sentences) to be ranked. The algorithm measures the similarity between the sentences and attaches a ranking score to each one of them.

Figure 3 shows MOOBO's interface and a short example of dialogue.

3 Evaluation

The system was evaluated with humans through a task-based evaluation, followed by a questionnaire. There were 18 participants recruited who are all undergraduate students at Edinburgh Napier University (so they were all familiar with the standard Moodle). Each participant was given a general overview of MOOBO and time to interact with the system. Each user was tasked to perform a set of pre-defined tasks using MOOBO and then using the standard Moodle. Specifically, the participants had to find information regarding the following:

1. The lab summary for "fundamentals of parallel systems" in week 2.
2. The coursework for "computational intelligence".
3. The deadline for the "Algorithms and Data structures" module.
4. The program leader for the "Design Dialogues" module.

After finishing these tasks, the participants were given a short questions (see Table 3.

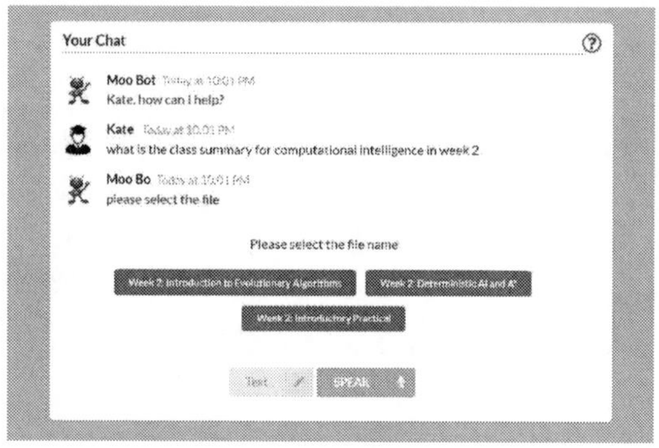

Figure 3: MOOBO's interface.

Questions
1. Was MOOBO accurate?
2. Was MOOBO easy to use?
3. Would you use MOOBO
4. Would you prefer using Moobo or a standard Moodle?
5. Overall how would you rate the experience? (0-bad, 10-excellent)

Table 3: List of questions answered by participants after completing the task-based evaluation.

4 Results and Discussion

The results showed that the participants really preferred MOOBO to standard Moodle. In fact, 76% of students said that it was accurate, 24% mentioned that it was accurate to an extent, adding that "I had to repeat a few times, but it was accurate afterwards" and "Sometimes it was unable to recognize what I said". Interestingly, none of the participants said that MOOBO was inaccurate.

All participants said that MOOBO was easy to use, which was expected given the widespread use of personal assistants nowadays as well as the participants' background. 71% of the users said they would use MOOBO, with 47% answering that they would use Moobo over Moodle. 24% stated they would use both, depending on the task and only 29% preferred the standard Moodle.

In the last question, students were asked to rate the overall experience from 0 to 10, where 0 is bad and 10 is excellent. The average rating was 8.5 ($mode = 8$, $median = 8$, no rating below 7 was given).

As seen from the results, Personal Assistants are positively seen by the users and they can speed up and ease performing specific tasks. Most students (76%) said that the answers were accurate which shows that the question was understood, and the Dialogue Manager selected the correct intent. However, there were some misunderstandings and MOOBO could not recognise the words or allocate the right task for the input. The second question received overwhelming responses. Every tester said it was easy to use MOOBO. This means that the designed user interface helped with the interaction. Extra features such as providing the link to a requested file and re-confirming if the question is correct were highly valued by users and helped them to access the information quicker. Personal Assistants become more popular and used, however they are not completely integrated with daily tasks.

5 Discussion and Conclusions

From the results presented, the following conclusions can be drawn for real-world NLG systems. Firstly, NLG NLG for interactive systems is an extremely challenging task. The main reason for this is that NLG is always influenced by other factors, such as natural language understanding, object recognition, human action recognition, dialogue management etc.

Secondly, NLG is quite domain-dependent, which requires access to example datasets of dialogues and interactions or access to experts. Both can be very expensive to acquire. By using approaches such as `one-shot learning` or even `zero-shot learning`(e.g. (Sadamitsu et al., 2017)) can help reducing the need of acquiring sizeable datasets. Our proposed setup can be extended to include visual information, which will enhance a robot's capability to monitor the environment and allow it to refer to objects in it as well as reason about it.

Finally, our toy example shows that we can approximate the state of the system by using embeddings. Pre-trained embeddings transfer knowledge from other domains to a new one and are especially useful in situations where only small datasets are available. This is an approach that can be transferred to human-robot communication. For instance, in situated setups, where a human and robot work together to accomplish a task such as assembling furniture, image and language embeddings can be used to approximate states, even if these states do not exist in the dataset.

6 Summary and Future Work

Acknowledgments

We are grateful to Edinburgh Napier University's technical team for granting us access to the university's Moodle environment as well as all the modules leaders who kindly shared and allowed us to use all their learning resources.

References

Rada Mihalcea and Paul Tarau. 2004. Textrank: Bringing order into text. In *Proceedings of the 2004 Conference on Empirical Methods in Natural Language Processing*.

Tomas Mikolov, Ilya Sutskever, Kai Chen, Greg Corrado, and Jeffrey Dean. 2013. Distributed representations of words and phrases and their compositionality. In *Neural and Information Processing System (NIPS)*.

Kugatsu Sadamitsu, Yukinori Homma, Ryuichiro Higashinaka, and Yoshihiro Matsuo. 2017. Zero-shot learning for natural language understanding using domain-independent sequential structure and question types. In *Proc. Interspeech 2017*, pages 3306–3310.

Florian Schroff, Dmitry Kalenichenko, and James Philbin. 2015. FaceNet: A Unified Embedding for Face Recognition and Clustering. pages 815–823.

Shaping a Social Robot's Humor with Natural Language Generation and Socially-Aware Reinforcement Learning

Hannes Ritschel and Elisabeth André
Human-Centered Multimedia, Augsburg University
Augsburg, Germany
{ritschel,andre}@hcm-lab.de

Abstract

Humor is an important aspect in human interaction to regulate conversations, increase interpersonal attraction and trust. For social robots, humor is one aspect to make interactions more natural, enjoyable, and to increase credibility and acceptance. In combination with appropriate non-verbal behavior, natural language generation offers the ability to create content on-the-fly. This work outlines the building-blocks for providing an individual, multimodal interaction experience by shaping the robot's humor with the help of Natural Language Generation and Reinforcement Learning based on human social signals.

1 Introduction

Humor is an important aspect in human interaction. It regulates conversations, increases interpersonal attraction and trust. For embodied conversational agents, including social robots, humor makes interactions more natural, enjoyable and increases credibility and acceptance (Nijholt, 2007). Canned jokes are the first type of humor that come to mind. In Human-Robot Interaction (HRI), they are used for entertainment purposes like stand-up comedy and joke telling. Moreover, there are several types of *conversational humor* (Dynel, 2009) which are employed in human conversation. Generation of such humorous contents from the computational perspective is hard because it usually requires human creativity, not only because it is often context-dependent. Several research projects already investigated generation of humor for chat bots and joke generation.

Natural Language Generation (NLG) is a key component for social robots to generate humorous contents on-the-fly, as it opens up the possibility to react to user input and to generate utterances without the need to prepare scripted content in advance. The expression of humor also requires to incorporate other modalities in the presentation, being mainly gestures, gaze and facial expressions.

Keeping the diversity of interaction contexts, tasks and human preferences in mind, social robots should not only express humor, but also adapt it accordingly. We propose an approach to realize this by combining NLG and Reinforcement Learning (RL) to adapt the robot to the individual user's preferences. Being able to dynamically generate and present humorous content in a multimodal manner is one step to explore how to increase perceived social intelligence and naturalness of interactions. As an example for the NLG part we focus on ironical contents here.

First, we outline related work covering humor from the perspective of language, gestures, gaze and facial expressions, as well as adaptive social robots. Afterwards, we look at how to implement expression of multimodal irony by combining NLG with non-verbal behaviors. Finally, we propose the use of RL in combination with human social signals to optimize parameters for aforementioned robot modalities automatically, resulting in personalized interaction experiences for the human user.

2 Related Work

We split up related work in two research areas: (1) computational humor and experiments, which investigate how to generate and present jokes, as well as the role of humor for robots (2) adaptation of social robots with focus on Reinforcement Learning.

Proceedings of the Workshop on NLG for Human–Robot Interaction, pages 12–16,
Tilburg, The Netherlands, November 8, 2018.

2.1 Humor

Several experiments for generation of humor in text form include e.g. the "Light Bulb Joke Generator" (Attardo and Raskin, 1994), "JAPE" and "STANDUP" for punning riddles (Binsted and Ritchie, 1997; Black et al., 2007) and "HAHACRONYM" for humorous acronyms (Stock and Strapparava, 2002), only to name a few. When looking at entertainment, Sjöbergh and Araki (2008) found that jokes presented by robots are rated significantly funnier than their text-only equivalents. Further scenarios include Japanese Manzai (Hayashi et al., 2008), stand-up comedy (Nijholt, 2018; Knight, 2011; Katevas et al., 2015) and joke telling (Weber et al., 2018), where the robot presents scripted contents to the audience. Apart from canned jokes, there are many types of *conversational humor* (Dynel, 2009). For embodied conversational agents, humor is one aspect which contributes to the naturalness of an interaction: it can help to solve communication problems and to increase acceptance of natural language interfaces when used sparingly and carefully (Binsted et al., 1995). Appropriateness plays an important role, as humor will yield misunderstanding in the wrong situation (Nijholt, 2007).

In the context of robots, research by Mirnig et al. (2016) comes to the conclusion that positively attributed forms of humor (self-irony) are rated significantly higher than negative ones (Schadenfreude) when it comes to robot likability. Their results also indicate a general positive effect of humor and an interaction effect between user personality and preferred type of humor. Results from recent studies by Mirnig et al. (2017) indicate that adding unimodal verbal or non-verbal, humorous elements to non-humorous robot behavior does not automatically result in increased perceived funniness. They point out that humor is multilayered and results from several modalities.

2.2 Social Adaptation

Social robots, which adapt their behaviors to human users, are used in a variety of settings. Aly and Tapus (2016) employ NLG with a NAO robot for user-robot personality matching. Both gestures and speech are adapted to the human's personality profile while the user can get information about several restaurants from the robot. Another approach is used by Tapus et al. (2008): the authors use RL to optimize the robot's personality in the context of post-stroke rehabilitation therapy. They use scripted utterances in the context of exercises.

RL is used often as machine learning framework for adaptation of social robots' behaviors. For example, it is used to learn social behavior (Barraquand and Crowley, 2008), for student tutoring (Gordon et al., 2016), to maintain long-term user engagement when playing games (Leite et al., 2011) and intervention for children with autism spectrum disorder (Liu et al., 2008).

Different data is used to provide the RL feedback signal (reward), including task-related information like user performance (e.g. in exercises/games) and human social signals. Tactile (Barraquand and Crowley, 2008) or prosodic (Kim and Scassellati, 2007) feedback, interaction distance, gaze meeting, motion speed, timing (Mitsunaga et al., 2008), gesture and posture (Najar et al., 2016; Ritschel et al., 2017), or gaze direction (Fournier et al., 2017) are used in different scenarios. Another option is to use physiological data from ECG (Liu et al., 2008) or EEG (Tsiakas et al., 2018). In the context of humor, smile and gaze (Leite et al., 2011; Gordon et al., 2016; Hemminghaus and Kopp, 2017), as well as laughter (Hayashi et al., 2008; Knight, 2011; Katevas et al., 2015; Weber et al., 2018) are used, as these are contemporary human reactions serving as an indication whether a joke is good or bad from the perspective of the human listener.

3 Adaptive Robot Humor with NLG

To shape the humor of a social robot, both humorous content as well as an adaptation approach to the human's preferences is presented. Since language plays an important role for communicating information, we take a look at NLG for generating ironical statements, combined with multimodal markers including facial expression, gaze or gestures. In combination, these can result in humorous contents and elicit human social signals, which can serve as indication whether the robot's behavior is pleasing or not.

3.1 Generating Ironical Statements

Computational creation of creative, humorous content is very hard. However, there are many findings concerning types and multimodal markers of humor (Burgers and van Mulken, 2017), especially for irony (Attardo et al., 2003), which can result in humor, too. We focus on ironical con-

Figure 1: Generating ironical statements in multiple stages

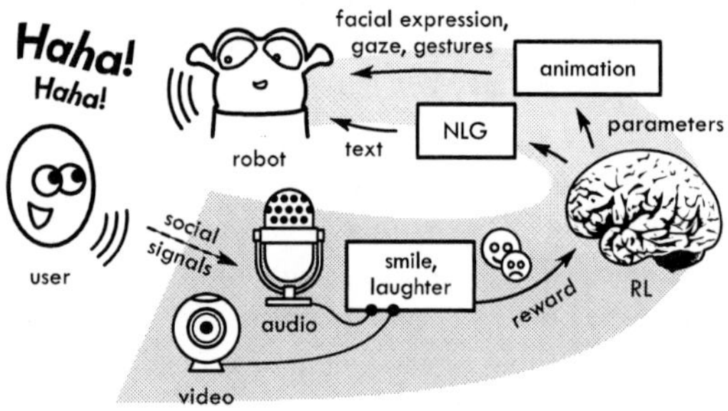

Figure 2: Overview of the adaptation process

tents here because the generation task can be realized as illustrated in Figure 1. First, Natural Language Processing (NLP) is used to check whether the input utterance can be transformed in an ironical statement. Then, NLG allows to convert the original utterance by inverting and applying linguistic markers. Apart from the semantic content of an ironical utterance, the way in which it is presented plays a crucial role. While written text may use direct, typographic or morpho-syntactic markers to help the reader to identify ironical content, linguistic, paralinguistic and visual markers are of special interest. Finally, these should be expressed by a robot with non-verbal behavior. Otherwise, irony might not be perceived by the listener. Facial expressions that indicate irony include raised or lowered eyebrows, wide open eyes, squinting or rolling, winking, nodding, smiling or a "blank face". Moreover, there are different acoustic parameter modulations. However, these are not consistent and differ from language to language.

The mentioned findings form a good starting point to implement expressive multimodal humorous contents for social robots by emphasizing spoken words generated by NLG with matching gaze, facial expressions and gestures in real-time.

3.2 Adaptation Process

Adaptation of humorous contents is often based on human social signals, primarily by sensing vocal laughter and smile to estimate the spectator's amusement. This applies to the aforementioned Japanese Manzai, standup comedy and joke telling scenarios. These experiments adapt the presented contents and their delivery in terms of animation, sound or voice parameters, but without generating content on-the-fly with the help of NLG.

Figure 2 outlines our suggested adaptation mechanism for learning about which humor the user prefers. It is based on the general idea of including human social signals in the learning process of the robot (Ritschel, 2018). The user's social signals are captured via camera and microphone. Signal processing allows to extract user smile and vocal laughter, similar to the operationalization in Weber et al. (2018). This information can be used to shape the reward of the machine learning process. RL is used to manipulate the generation of the humorous content by altering parameters for NLG and animation, e.g. resulting in the use of ironical comments in one situation or not. Actually, there are many options what actually can be learned, including humor types or parameters of animation generation, e.g. to optimize non-verbal aspects of joke presentation, which might have different effects when expressed by a robot than by a human. By incorporating the user's feedback in terms of smile and laughter, the agent is able to learn how to make the user laugh by means of language, facial expression, gaze or gestures. Combining NLG with the generation of additional multimodal behaviors allows social robots to add humorous elements in conversations. It provides the opportunity to personalize and adapt the interaction experience to the individual preferences of the human user.

4 Conclusion

We have outlined the important role and opportunities of NLG to increase the credibility and acceptance of the robot and the naturalness of interactions. Generating contents on-the-fly allows to add humorous elements on demand. We have described an adaptation process to realize individualized interaction experiences for the human user. By incorporating human social signals in the RL process the robot can optimize the presentation of humorous contents depending on interaction context, task and human preferences.

Acknowledgments

This research was funded by the Bavarian State Ministry for Education, Science and the Arts (STMWFK) as part of the ForGenderCare research association, as well as by the Deutsche Forschungsgemeinschaft (DFG) within the project "How to Win Arguments - Empowering Virtual Agents to Improve their Persuasiveness", Grant Number 376696351, as part of the Priority Program "Robust Argumentation Machines (RATIO)" (SPP-1999).

References

2016. *25th IEEE International Symposium on Robot and Human Interactive Communication, RO-MAN 2016, New York, NY, USA, August 26-31, 2016*. IEEE.

Amir Aly and Adriana Tapus. 2016. Towards an intelligent system for generating an adapted verbal and nonverbal combined behavior in human-robot interaction. *Auton. Robots*, 40(2):193–209.

Salvatore Attardo, Jodi Eisterhold, Jennifer Hay, and Isabella Poggi. 2003. Multimodal markers of irony and sarcasm. *Humor*, 16(2):243–260.

Salvatore Attardo and Jonathan D Raskin. 1994. Nonliteralness and non-bona-fide in language: An approach to formal and computational treatments of humor. *Pragmatics & Cognition*, 2(1):31–69.

Rémi Barraquand and James L. Crowley. 2008. Learning polite behavior with situation models. In *Proceedings of the 3rd ACM/IEEE international conference on Human robot interaction, HRI 2008, Amsterdam, The Netherlands, March 12-15, 2008*, pages 209–216. ACM.

Kim Binsted and Graeme Ritchie. 1997. Computational rules for generating punning riddles. *HUMOR-International Journal of Humor Research*, 10(1):25–76.

Kim Binsted et al. 1995. Using humour to make natural language interfaces more friendly. In *Proceedings of the AI, ALife and Entertainment Workshop, Intern. Joint Conf. on Artificial Intelligence*.

Rolf Black, Annalu Waller, Graeme Ritchie, Helen Pain, and Ruli Manurung. 2007. Evaluation of joke-creation software with children with complex communication needs. In *Communication Matters*. Citeseer.

Christian Burgers and Margot van Mulken. 2017. Humor markers. *The Routledge handbook of language and humor*, pages 385–399.

Marta Dynel. 2009. Beyond a joke: Types of conversational humour. *Language and Linguistics Compass*, 3(5):1284–1299.

Pierre Fournier, Olivier Sigaud, and Mohamed Chetouani. 2017. Combining artificial curiosity and tutor guidance for environment exploration. In *Workshop on Behavior Adaptation, Interaction and Learning for Assistive Robotics at IEEE RO-MAN 2017*.

Goren Gordon, Samuel Spaulding, Jacqueline Kory Westlund, Jin Joo Lee, Luke Plummer, Marayna Martinez, Madhurima Das, and Cynthia Breazeal. 2016. Affective personalization of a social robot tutor for children's second language skills. In *Proceedings of the Thirtieth AAAI Conference on Artificial Intelligence, February 12-17, 2016, Phoenix, Arizona, USA.*, pages 3951–3957. AAAI Press.

Kotaro Hayashi, Takayuki Kanda, Takahiro Miyashita, Hiroshi Ishiguro, and Norihiro Hagita. 2008. Robot *Manzai*: Robot conversation as a passive-social medium. *I. J. Humanoid Robotics*, 5(1):67–86.

Jacqueline Hemminghaus and Stefan Kopp. 2017. Towards adaptive social behavior generation for assistive robots using reinforcement learning. In *Proceedings of the 2017 ACM/IEEE International Conference on Human-Robot Interaction, HRI 2017, Vienna, Austria, March 6-9, 2017*, pages 332–340. ACM.

Kleomenis Katevas, Patrick GT Healey, and Matthew Tobias Harris. 2015. Robot comedy lab: experimenting with the social dynamics of live performance. *Frontiers in psychology*, 6.

E. S. Kim and B. Scassellati. 2007. Learning to refine behavior using prosodic feedback. In *2007 IEEE 6th International Conference on Development and Learning*, pages 205–210.

Heather Knight. 2011. Eight lessons learned about non-verbal interactions through robot theater. In *Social Robotics - Third International Conference, ICSR 2011, Amsterdam, The Netherlands, November 24-25, 2011. Proceedings*, volume 7072 of *Lecture Notes in Computer Science*, pages 42–51. Springer.

Iolanda Leite, André Pereira, Ginevra Castellano, Samuel Mascarenhas, Carlos Martinho, and Ana Paiva. 2011. Modelling empathy in social robotic companions. In *Advances in User Modeling - UMAP 2011 Workshops, Girona, Spain, July 11-15, 2011, Revised Selected Papers*, volume 7138 of *Lecture Notes in Computer Science*, pages 135–147. Springer.

Changchun Liu, Karla Conn, Nilanjan Sarkar, and Wendy Stone. 2008. Online affect detection and robot behavior adaptation for intervention of children with autism. *IEEE Trans. Robotics*, 24(4):883–896.

Nicole Mirnig, Susanne Stadler, Gerald Stollnberger, Manuel Giuliani, and Manfred Tscheligi. 2016. Robot humor: How self-irony and schadenfreude influence people's rating of robot likability. In (DBL, 2016), pages 166–171.

Nicole Mirnig, Gerald Stollnberger, Manuel Giuliani, and Manfred Tscheligi. 2017. Elements of humor: How humans perceive verbal and non-verbal aspects of humorous robot behavior. In *Companion of the 2017 ACM/IEEE International Conference on Human-Robot Interaction, HRI 2017, Vienna, Austria, March 6-9, 2017*, pages 211–212. ACM.

Noriaki Mitsunaga, Christian Smith, Takayuki Kanda, Hiroshi Ishiguro, and Norihiro Hagita. 2008. Adapting robot behavior for human–robot interaction. *IEEE Trans. Robotics*, 24(4):911–916.

Anis Najar, Olivier Sigaud, and Mohamed Chetouani. 2016. Training a robot with evaluative feedback and unlabeled guidance signals. In (DBL, 2016), pages 261–266.

Anton Nijholt. 2007. *Conversational Agents and the Construction of Humorous Acts*, chapter 2. Wiley-Blackwell.

Anton Nijholt. 2018. Robotic stand-up comedy: State-of-the-art. In *Distributed, Ambient and Pervasive Interactions: Understanding Humans - 6th International Conference, DAPI 2018, Held as Part of HCI International 2018, Las Vegas, NV, USA, July 15-20, 2018, Proceedings, Part I*, volume 10921 of *Lecture Notes in Computer Science*, pages 391–410. Springer.

Hannes Ritschel. 2018. Socially-aware reinforcement learning for personalized human-robot interaction. In *Proceedings of the 17th International Conference on Autonomous Agents and MultiAgent Systems, AAMAS 2018, Stockholm, Sweden, July 10-15, 2018*, pages 1775–1777. International Foundation for Autonomous Agents and Multiagent Systems Richland, SC, USA / ACM.

Hannes Ritschel, Tobias Baur, and Elisabeth André. 2017. Adapting a robot's linguistic style based on socially-aware reinforcement learning. In *26th IEEE International Symposium on Robot and Human Interactive Communication, RO-MAN 2017, Lisbon, Portugal, August 28 - Sept. 1, 2017*, pages 378–384. IEEE.

Jonas Sjöbergh and Kenji Araki. 2008. Robots make things funnier. In *New Frontiers in Artificial Intelligence, JSAI 2008 Conference and Workshops, Asahikawa, Japan, June 11-13, 2008, Revised Selected Papers*, volume 5447 of *Lecture Notes in Computer Science*, pages 306–313. Springer.

Oliviero Stock and Carlo Strapparava. 2002. Hahacronym: Humorous agents for humorous acronyms. *Stock, Oliviero, Carlo Strapparava, and Anton Nijholt. Eds*, pages 125–135.

Adriana Tapus, Cristian Tapus, and Maja J. Mataric. 2008. User - robot personality matching and assistive robot behavior adaptation for post-stroke rehabilitation therapy. *Intelligent Service Robotics*, 1(2):169–183.

Konstantinos Tsiakas, Maher Abujelala, and Fillia Makedon. 2018. Task engagement as personalization feedback for socially-assistive robots and cognitive training. *Technologies*, 6(2).

Klaus Weber, Hannes Ritschel, Ilhan Aslan, Florian Lingenfelser, and Elisabeth André. 2018. How to shape the humor of a robot - social behavior adaptation based on reinforcement learning. In *Proceedings of the 2018 on International Conference on Multimodal Interaction, ICMI 2018, Boulder, CO, USA, October 16-20, 2018*, pages 154–162. ACM.

From Sensors to Sense: Integrated Heterogeneous Ontologies for Natural Language Generation

Mihai Pomarlan and **Robert Porzel** and **John Bateman** and **Rainer Malaka***
University of Bremen
{pomarlan, bateman}@uni-bremen.de {porzel, malaka}@tzi.de

Abstract

We propose the combination of a robotics ontology (KnowRob) with a linguistically motivated one (GUM) under the upper ontology DUL. We use the DUL Event, Situation, Description pattern to formalize reasoning techniques to convert between a robot's beliefstate and its linguistic utterances. We plan to employ these techniques to equip robots with a *reason-aloud* ability, through which they can explain their actions as they perform them, in natural language, at a level of granularity appropriate to the user, their query and the context at hand.

1 Introduction

It is a sunny afternoon in the not too distant future, and Elroy wants to play ball in the garden with Rosie the robot. He finds her moving about in the dining room and asks "What are you doing?". "I am busy", Rosie answers, politely but suggesting she doesn't want to be interrupted right now. Disappointed, but not wanting to let go just yet, Elroy presses on. "What are you doing?" he asks again. "I am setting the table," Rosie answers. Still not satified he repeats his question again and Rosie explains "I am bringing cutlery and plates to the table and currently looking in this cupboard for a spoon and fork for Judy. They must not be plastic, for she is allergic to it."

The little scene above shows an interaction between a human and a household robot where the appropriate level of granularity with which the robot should describe its task varies greatly as the dialog situation evolves. Generally, such interactions cannot be restricted to command-giving (by the human) and command-taking (by the robot). Even a specialized device, e.g. a coffee machine, offers some feedback about its state. Indeed, the spectrum of possible interactions can be quite complex: the robot might ask for a way around an obstacle it encountered in a task, discuss user preferences and task schedules, take initiative in asking for parameters of upcoming tasks, or ask the users about their activities, as these will affect the robot's task planning and execution.

Compared to more complex situations, the one in our example scene seems simple, but it nevertheless captures an aspect that will be important for the interlocutionary capabilities of robots: the ability to interpret events and to describe them understandably, at a level of granularity appropriate for the user and their query. This requires integrating heterogeneous forms of knowledge, such as records of sensor data, representations of activities at different abstraction levels, and theories about the environment and the interlocutionary partners.

For this undertaking, we envision a *reason-aloud* capability for robotic agents, analogous to human *think-aloud*. Humans are quite capable of reflecting overtly on their actions and describing them in parallel to their execution, which is why the *think aloud protocol* has become widely used in numerous studies in cognitive science, psychology and human-computer interaction (van Someren and Barnard, 1994). For this a situated artificial agent must combine knowledge of the activities at hand with the knowledge required to express them declaratively.

*This work was partially funded by Deutsche Forschungsgemeinschaft (DFG) through the Collaborative Research Center 1320, EASE.

Proceedings of the Workshop on NLG for Human–Robot Interaction, pages 17–21,
Tilburg, The Netherlands, November 8, 2018.

2 Approach

Our approach is to extend an Ontology for Everyday Activities, originally developed as part of the EASE project in robotics (Beetz et al., 2018). We base this extended ontology on the principles proposed by Masolo *et al.* using the DOLCE+DnS Ultralite ontology (DUL) as an overarching foundational framework (Masolo et al., 2003; Mascardi et al., 2010). The purpose of the ontology is to extend the KnowRob ontology to support more natural, commonsense interactions concerning everyday activities in robotics. Specific branches of the KnowRob knowledge model pertaining to everyday activities (Beetz et al., 2018), such as those involved in table setting, have already been aligned to the DUL framework. Additional axiomatization that is beyond the scope of description logics is integrated by means of the Distributed Ontology Language (Mossakowski, 2016). The extension we consider in this paper is for adding language generation capabilities, to which end we align the linguistically motivated ontology GUM (Bateman et al., 2010), and its extension to spatial concepts, to DUL and the EASE ontology.

The key advantage of this ontological alignment via DUL is first and foremost a bridge between the KnowRob system, a mature knowledge processing system for robotics (see section 3) and language generation software that uses GUM representations, such as KPML (Bateman, 1997). Using the DUL-specific *Descriptions and Situations* pattern, we can employ these to supply concepts and reasoning methods for the problem of interpreting `Events` into `Situations` and constructing `Descriptions` for them (see section 4.1).

We will only look at command-taking and the robot performing a "reasoning aloud" (analogous to human "think aloud") in this paper. We hope the reasoning techniques enabled by our approach will lay a scalable base for future work on more complex interactions, e.g. dialogical negotiating when activities conflict, but we stress that a "reasoning aloud" capability can be useful on its own. It shows understanding on the robot's part of the task it performs, and makes the robot itself more understandable to the user.

3 KnowRob and KPML

KnowRob (Beetz et al., 2018) is a software system to integrate and reason with a variety of robotics knowledge sources. Its interface is a database query system via Prolog predicates, providing a uniform way to access the reasoning mechanisms underneath. These mechanisms can, however, be varied by employing an approach called *computables* which allows for predicates to map to and take results from functions appropriate for a task.

In this way, KnowRob can do hybrid reasoning on symbolic data - which it queries or infers from a logical database - as well as raw data - such as sensor readings and log files. Reasoning mechanisms can make use of logical axioms, but also perform collision or visibility testing in an environment and draw on inverse kinematics, physical simulation, etc. To handle uncertainty, KnowRob uses probabilistic, first-order relational models. These models are intended to capture general principles about similar objects. For example, they may represent a probability distribution on where to look for an item, or where to store it in a kitchen, given its type.

To handle environment dynamics, the KnowRob ontology includes some concepts for Actions and their Effects. We have extended the ontology's coverage in this respect and brought it into alignment with DUL. Also, the KnowRob ontology defines concepts that have been used to construct what are termed within the EASE project as NEEMs (Narratively Enabled Episodic Memories), which are comprehensive records of a robot's activity: this includes what the robot has observed through its sensors, how it acted in the world, its task tree (from which a hierarchy of *intentions* is discernible) and the execution status of tasks. KnowRob contains predicates to select and reason with `Events` recorded in the NEEMs, including temporal calculi. NEEMs were intended as data collection for learning, to improve robot performance. Expert users can employ them to debug the robot. On their own however, they are too large and incomprehensible for the average user to handle, making natural language techniques highly relevant.

For generating comprehensible and appropriate language we propose to employ KPML. This system offers a well-tested platform for grammar engineering that is specifically designed for natural language generation (Reiter and Dale, 2000). KPML employs the use of large-scale grammars written with the framework of Systemic-Functional Linguistics (SFL). The employment of SFL enables us to include linguistic phenomena which are important for the generation of natural texts alongside the propositional content that is to be expressed (Bateman, 1997).

In the following, we will outline how the respective interleaving of the symbolic layers of KnowRob and the ontological model of GUM via DUL facilitates crossing the bridge from a robot executing particular actions to talking about them in real time. As stated before, we also are working on using the same bridge to enable the robot to understand linguistic input, i.e. instructions.

4 From Language to Beliefstate– and back again

4.1 Event, Situation, Description

We will first summarize a few DUL concepts that are central to our approach. `Events` are either `Processes` or `States`, in which several objects may participate. An `Event` is related to one or more `Situations`, which are *views* on (or interpretations of) an `Event`. A `Situation` satisfies, or is consistent with, a `Description`. As an example, a robot's movements and the contacts between objects that they cause would be events. A situation would be the robot executing a plan for table setting. The table setting plan itself would be the description consistent with the situation.

A robot's knowledge cuts across all these distinctions. The robot causes, observes, and records events as they happen. It may be situated as executing a task, or interacting with a user towards some purpose. And it has theories of the environment around itself, e.g. action, environment, and user models, as well as higher-level plans.

Most generally, communication between user and robot involves the two exchanging descriptions, for which we identify two problems:

- command/inform: the robot receives a linguistic description. It creates new descriptions and situations as appropriate so as to update its belief state about the world or begin executing a requested task.
- reason aloud: the robot has a record of events, a representation of the situations it is in, and various descriptions. It summarizes this knowledge into a description, to answer a query at an appropriate level of granularity, without overwhelming the user.

The purpose of our combined ontology is to enable reasoning techniques to bridge these conversions: events to situations, and situations to descriptions. All the more specific components are consequently related to the DUL backbone.

4.2 Events ↔ Situations

The direction especially relevant for us here is going from events to situations that interpret them. The opposite, from situations to events, means simply that the robot causes events in the world according to some chosen plan. For this purpose, we define several classes of situations in our ontology, with restrictions to specify when it is appropriate to use the situation as an interpretation for the set of events. Several situations may be appropriate to interpret a set of events. Situations include:

- an agent (human/robot) acting on inanimate objects, e.g. 'Actor Creates Something', 'Actor Affects Something', 'Resource Absent'.
- human-robot interaction, e.g. 'Command Issued', 'Availability Query'.
- inanimate objects acting on each other, e.g. 'Stable Placement', 'Physical Interaction'.

Usually, choosing an interpretation when the robot is the only active agent in the events is straightforward; the robot "knows" what its task tree is, i.e., what it wants to do, because for the robotic system we use the programs it runs are semantically annotated with goals.

Finding an appropriate situation in other cases either implies guessing the other agent's intentions, for which probabilistic reasoning or simulation can be used to find the most likely intentions given the observed evidence, or, if there is no active agent in the event, parsing an event timeline according to a grammar of situations (cf. (Beßler et al., 2018b) for an action parser using the DUL and KnowRob ontologies).

4.3 Situations ↔ Descriptions

We will first look at describing a situation to the user. Some situation classes in our ontology have unique description correspondents, e.g., "Actor Creates Something" has GUM's "CreativeMaterialAction", while others may define, via restrictions, subsets of descriptions applicable to them.

To construct description individuals – filling in semantic roles – we use a method employed in KnowRob for assembly planning (Beßler et al., 2018a) which checks that an individual asserted to belong to a class actually respects restrictions placed on that class, in particular whether it is linked to other individuals by appropriate object properties. If this is not the case, the method creates new individuals and relations as needed. Restrictions on fillers for a description's semantic frame roles can be written in SWRL.

We will also investigate reasoning methods to update the interaction situation in the robot's beliefstate based on user utterances. These will be semantically analyzed and interpreted as commands or queries. For commands, robot programs will be constructed using blocks from a library of basic actions. Query answering involves the event-situation-description bridges described previously.

As an example of how our approach is intended to work, consider the following scenario: the robot has *"setting the table"* as its top-level task, and it knows this task is intended to prepare another task (*"eating"*) to be done by other agents. The current subtask the robot is performing is *"picking"* a spoon. Note, mechanisms to represent and reason about task trees are already in place in our knowledge processing system.

Suppose the robot decides to report that it is *"setting the table"*, which is a particular type of situation captured by a broad situation concept AgentAffectsSomething. Our ontological characterization is that a AgentAffectsSomething individual satisfies some gum-DispositiveMaterialAction, so we create an individual of this latter type to describe what the robot is doing.

Individuals of type gum-DispositiveMaterialAction should obey certain restrictions however. One such restriction is such an individual should have an actor that is some GUMThing, and our newly created individual has no such information attached yet. To enforce this restriction, an agenda item is generated to create and look for a suitable actor, which in this case will be a description of the agent of the *"setting the table"* situation.

Where needed one can go beyond restrictions placed on descriptions in the GUM. For example, suppose we want the robot to say why it is *"setting the table"*. In this case, we add a new restriction on the newly created gum-DispositiveMaterialAction individual, that it should have as reason some GUMThing, and this will result in an agenda item to look for a filler for this role, which will be a description of the task that *"setting the table"* prepares.

What the user should be told as part of a "think-aloud" protocol depends on what the robot thinks the user might know about the robot's task, so let's suppose as an example the user knows nothing. The question then is what to report from the task tree, which will probably have very many nodes? Several heuristics may be tried here, but they can be formulated in terms of the task tree structure. One such heuristic is to report the current subtask, *"picking"*, the robot's top-level task, *"setting the table"*, and the task being prepared by the robot's top-level task, *"eating"*.

Each of these situations gets a Description individual of appropriate GUM type. There is flexibility in choosing which of the three gets to be the main clause of the resulting utterance and which get to be dependents, which offers us flexibility in generating a report:

```
I'm picking up the spoon because I'm
  setting the table so people can eat.
I'm setting the table because people will
  eat, therefore I'm picking up the spoon.
People will eat soon therefore I'm setting
  the table so I'm picking up the spoon.
```

4.4 Matching the Description Granularity

There may be several parses of a set of events, several situations that are possible views on them, and several descriptions for each situation; e.g., levels of abstraction at which to report in the reasoning aloud. Fortunately, the graphs representing the situations already feature different levels of generality. For example, a situation where we encounter a "grasp - lift - place - release" pattern will be categorized as a "pick and place" action, which, in turn, can be part of a more general activity such as "table setting". The hierarchy and the respective distances in the graph has to be aligned to the information stemming from the interaction situation to pick out which level of abstraction to report.

Numerous approaches have been proposed to control such alignments. Very prominent in natural language generation are approaches based on user modeling, e.g. the TAILOR system (Paris, 1988). However, also discourse modeling (Pfleger et al., 2003) or the situational context (Porzel, 2009) come into play when selecting the propositional level of granularity. Formally, levels of granularity can also be expressed as a set of theories forming a hierarchical structure (Hobbs, 1985). Nevertheless, a concrete method for matching these structures has to be found and tested.

References

John Bateman. 1997. *Enabling technology for multilingual natural language generation: the KPML development environment*, volume 3(1):15–55. Journal of Natural Language Engineering.

John A. Bateman, Joana Hois, Robert J. Ross, and Thora Tenbrink. 2010. A linguistic ontology of space for natural language processing. *Artificial Intelligence*, 174(14):1027–1071.

Michael Beetz, Daniel Beßler, Andrei Haidu, Mihai Pomarlan, Asil Kaan Bozcuoglu, and Georg Bartels. 2018. Knowrob 2.0 – a 2nd generation knowledge processing framework for cognition-enabled robotic agents. In *International Conference on Robotics and Automation (ICRA)*, Brisbane, Australia.

Daniel Beßler, Mihai Pomarlan, and Michael Beetz. 2018a. Owl-enabled assembly planning for robotic agents. In *Proceedings of the 2018 International Conference on Autonomous Agents*, AAMAS '18, Stockholm, Sweden. Finalist for the Best Robotics Paper Award.

Daniel Beßler, Robert Porzel, Mihai Pomarlan, Hagen Langer, John Bateman, Rainer Malaka, and Michael Beetz. 2018b. Foundational models for manipulation activity parsing. In *Proceedings of the 2018 International Conference on Robotics and Automation (ICRA) (submitted for review)*.

Jerry R. Hobbs. 1985. Granularity. In *Proceedings of the 9th International Joint Conference on Artificial Intelligence - Volume 1*, IJCAI'85, pages 432–435, San Francisco, CA, USA. Morgan Kaufmann Publishers Inc.

Viviana Mascardi, Valentina Cord, and Paolo Rosso. 2010. Technical report disi-tr-06-21, university of genua.

C Masolo, Stefano Borgo, Aldo Gangemi, Nicola Guarino, and A Oltramari. 2003. Wonderweb deliverable d18 ontology library.

Till Mossakowski. 2016. The distributed ontology, model and specification language - DOL. In *Recent Trends in Algebraic Development Techniques - 23rd IFIP WG 1.3 International Workshop, WADT 2016, Gregynog, UK, September 21-24, 2016, Revised Selected Papers*, pages 5–10.

Cécile L. Paris. 1988. Tailoring object descriptions to a user's level of expertise. *Comput. Linguist.*, 14(3):64–78.

Norbert Pfleger, Jan Alexandersson, and Tilman Becker. 2003. A robust and generic discourse model for multimodal dialogue. In *Proceedings of the 3rd Workshop on Knowledge and Reasoning In Practical Dialogue Systems*.

Robert Porzel. 2009. *Contextual computing for natural language processing*. Ph.D. thesis, University of Bremen.

Ehud Reiter and Robert Dale. 2000. *Building Natural Language Generation Systems*. Cambridge University Press, Cambridge, U.K.

Maarten van Someren and Yvonne Barnard. 1994. *THE THINK ALOUD METHOD: A practical guide to modelling cognitive processes*. Academic Press, London, U.K.

A Farewell to Arms: Non-verbal Communication for Non-humanoid Robots*

Aaron G. Cass
Union College
Schenectady, NY, USA
cassa@union.edu

Kristina Striegnitz
Union College
Schenectady, NY, USA
striegnk@union.edu

Nick Webb
Union College
Schenectady, NY, USA
webbn@union.edu

Abstract

Human-robot interactions situated in a dynamic environment create a unique mix of challenges for conversational systems. We argue that, on the one hand, NLG can contribute to addressing these challenges and that, on the other hand, they pose interesting research problems for NLG. To illustrate our position we describe our research on non-humanoid robots using non-verbal signals to support communication.

1 Introduction

Our research is about interaction strategies for robots who have to approach and communicate with strangers in busy public spaces (Cass et al., 2015, 2018). For example, in one of our target scenarios a delivery robot in a busy academic building on a college campus has to solicit help to operate the elevator from humans passing by. In another scenario a robot is recruiting survey participants in a shopping mall. In order to develop solutions that will work in a real-world deployment, we collect data and study human-robot interaction not just in laboratory experiments but also in field studies conducted in the wild.

In these field studies we have encountered challenges that are traditionally not addressed by the natural language generation (NLG) pipeline. However, we would like to argue that an NLG system aware of these issues can contribute to a better solution and that they also pose interesting research problems for NLG.

In particular, the following two sources of challenges have stood out to us. First, the robot is situated in a dynamic environment with human interaction partners that can act while the robot is speaking or planning an utterance. As in other situated communication tasks (Koller et al., 2010; Smith et al., 2011) the timing of the robot's utterances is important. For fluent interactions the robot needs to monitor the human's actions and changes in the environment and react to them in a timely manner, potentially by interrupting itself or modifying an utterance mid-stream (Clark and Krych, 2004).

Second, many environmental factors may hinder communication and are not controllable by us or the robot. For example, in a busy public space the background noise level may be high, making it hard for people to hear the robot. People may be passing by and even in between the robot and the addressee. The robot will encounter many different reactions from addressees; some will be surprised, scared, or embarrassed to interact with it.

One approach to these challenges would be to solve these issues first in order to create a situation where a "traditional" NLG pipeline, based on NLG for text generation, can be used optimally. For example, we could try to develop a module that perfectly times utterances, make sure to adjust the audio level to always be above the environmental noise level, and only communicate with addressees that are directly in front of the robot. However, these goals may be impossible to achieve. For example, while it makes sense to optimize the timing of utterances, most contributing factors are out of our control, so that the robot will always have to be prepared to deal with unexpected actions by the human addressee, changes in the environment, or network delays. Furthermore, this approach may lead to suboptimal results. For instance, if the robot only communicates with people if they are positioned right in front of it, in a busy space with people passing through, many opportunities for interaction may be lost.

Therefore, we believe that NLG should be

*Position paper presented at the workshop on natural language generation for human-robot communication at INLG 2018.

Proceedings of the Workshop on NLG for Human–Robot Interaction, pages 22–26,
Tilburg, The Netherlands, November 8, 2018.

aware of these issues and can contribute to a solution. For example: An incremental NLG module may be able to better time utterances and react to unexpected changes (Allen et al., 2001; Buschmeier et al., 2012). When the environment is noisy or the robot is far away from the addressee, generating shorter utterances using simpler words and complementing speech with non-verbal signals might be more effective. Previous work has explored the problem of adapting the form and content of generated utterances to situational constraints (e.g. Jokinen and Wilcock, 2003; Walker et al., 2007; Rieser et al., 2014), but typically not in the context of human-robot interaction.

In order to illustrate our position, we will describe some results and observations from our ongoing research on making human-robot communication more robust using non-verbal signals. A lot of work has been done on generating non-verbal signals, like gestures, facial expressions, and posture for animated characters (known as embodied conversational agents or virtual humans). Some of this work has been transferred to humanoid robots. However, because of our application scenario, the use of humanoid robots is not practical for us. We need robots that are tall enough to interact with standing humans and that are not too expensive to be deployed in a busy public space. We work with robots that have a wheeled base and a mounted screen (see Figure 1).

The research challenge is, therefore, to find out what non-verbal signals are effective communicative devices for these non-humanoid robots. These signals may mimic human behaviors, or they may be visual metaphors that express the robot's intentions in a way that is not modeling realistic human behavior, similar to the way comics express a character's movement or emotions.

2 Related Work

People accompany their speech with non-verbal signals, which support and add to the content of the speech and which help manage the dialog. For example, iconic hand gestures may depict some features of an object or event being described (McNeill, 1992), eye gaze plays an important role in regulating turn-taking in dialog (Kendon, 1967), and facial displays express a speaker's emotions (Ekman and Friesen, 2003) but also serve pragmatic functions that help organize the dialog (Chovil, 1991).

Embodied conversational agents (ECAs) or virtual humans are animated characters that engage with humans in a dialog using both verbal and non-verbal communication (Cassell et al., 2000). Typical research in this area closely analyzes human non-verbal behavior and aims to model these behaviors in the animated character.

Some of this work on generating non-verbal behaviors for animated conversational characters has been transferred to physical humanoid robots. Salem et al. (2012) and Hasegawa et al. (2010) use gesture generation strategies developed for ECAs on humanoid robots. Breazeal (2000) presents a robot with a simple cartoonish face that can express emotions and interaction cues. Most expressions are modeled on human facial expressions. But the robot can also use its non-human, animal-like ears to indicate arousal and attention.

While Breazeal's (2000) work shows that even with humanoid robots going beyond the normal human repertoire of non-verbal signals can be beneficial, non-humanoid robots often are not capable of mimicking human non-verbal behaviors. It is therefore essential to identify what behaviors of non-humanoid robots can easily be interpreted by humans (Cha et al., 2018). Recent work has, for example, explored the interpretability of robot arm movements (Dragan et al., 2013). In a study that is most similar to our research, Cha and Matarić (2016) have shown that a service robot can use light and sound signals to indicate that it needs help and to communicate levels of urgency.

3 Experiments Exploring Non-verbal Signals for Non-humanoid robots

We describe three studies we have carried out or are currently conducting to explore how non-verbal behaviors can contribute to communication between humans and non-humanoid robots. In these studies we explore non-verbal robot behaviors modeled on human behaviors as well as robot behaviors designed to communicate metaphorically through movement.

The two robots we have used for this work, SARAH and VALERIE, both have a mobile base, a screen on which a simple cartoon face can be displayed, and a suite of cameras and depth sensors (VALERIE is shown in Figure 1). Importantly, the robots have a non-humanoid form, lacking the typical mechanisms for human non-verbal expression. Our experiments are conducted using

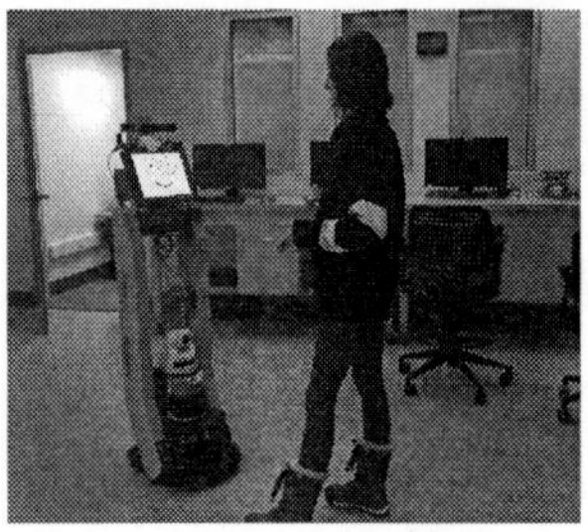

Figure 1: VALERIE

a Wizard of Oz (WoZ) protocol, in which a human wizard remotely controls the robot unbeknownst to the participants. The wizard interface provides a set of pre-planned behaviors the wizard can initiate, as well as lower-level controls for the robot.

3.1 Robot eye gaze to support reference

In this ongoing study we look at whether humans use our robot's eye gaze to resolve referring expressions. Hanna and Brennan (2007) found that humans use a human instruction giver's eye gaze to distinguish an object being described from its similar looking distractors. We replicated their experiment, in the laboratory, with VALERIE taking the instruction giver's place.

Participants stood opposite VALERIE with a table between them. On the table was a sequence of colored shapes, each of which also had a number of black dots. Some layouts contained distractor pairs, which are shapes of the same color and form, but with a different number of dots. VALERIE gave instructions of the form *"Press the button corresponding to the blue triangle with three dots"*, while either only moving her mouth or, additionally, accompanying the instruction by a movement of the pupils in the direction of the target shape. A preliminary analysis of the data suggests that VALERIE's eye gaze helps participants pick out the right target more quickly in situations where the layout contains a distractor shape that is sufficiently far away from the target shape that it can be distinguished by eye gaze.

This shows that the participants do indeed interpret the robot's eye gaze and use it to guide their own behavior. From an NLG point of view, the generation of eye gaze is interesting because eye gaze has to be coordinated with the natural language utterance it accompanies, while also producing natural looking eye movements.

Limitations and future work: This study was done in a laboratory environment using a repetitive and unrealistic task. We plan to conduct a follow up study that tests the effectiveness of robot eye gaze as a communicative device in the wild.

3.2 Robot body movement and orientation to attract attention and initiate interactions

In this experiment in the wild, the robot behavior was designed to (very crudely) mimic the behaviors humans might use to initiate an interaction with a passer-by in a busy public space. SARAH was stationed in a popular hallway. She would greet people ("Hello! Can you please help me?") either while standing still or accompanied by a rotational movement that followed the subject we wished to engage. People who approached SARAH were then asked to press a specific number on a keypad.

We collected video data of 14 one-hour sessions over the course of 5 weeks. In total, 1658 people passed by SARAH. Of those, only 714 engaged with her in any way, including just looking at her. Of the 714, 108 completed our task. We found that movement of the robot statistically significantly increased how many people looked at SARAH (64% of passers-by noticed the still robot, 88% the moving robot), but not the number of completed tasks (6.4% in the non-moving condition, 6.7% in the moving condition). Given a 30% increase in the number of people who notice SARAH, we expected a similar increase in the number of people who stop to interact with her.

A closer analysis of our video data indicates that technical issues with the WoZ interface (which we plan to address in follow-up experiments) as well as issues related to SARAH's communicative behavior may be the reason for why the increased attention did not lead to more successful interactions. First, it seems that SARAH's intentions weren't always clear and, second, several people in the study acted surprised or scared of SARAH or embarrassed to interact with her. Both issues point toward a need for better communicative nonverbal behaviors to convey the robot's intentions and to lessen people's apprehension.

As with eye gaze, these non-verbal behaviors have to be planned and coordinated with the robot's natural language utterances. An additional challenge is that the signals we are exploring are complex, involving eye gaze, facial expressions, and different kinds of movement. Furthermore, the optimal choice of non-verbal signals and form or natural language utterance may depend on aspects of the environment, such as how busy and noisy it is or how far away the addressee is. The NLG system planning these utterances will have to be able to coordinate diverse types of communicative signals and to adapt to the current situation.

Future work: In our current work, we are studying verbal and non-verbal behaviors that allow the robot to better signal its wish to interact (e.g. moving toward the selected addressee, facial expressions to indicate a need for help and a wish to engage). This exploration is guided by what is known about human behaviors in similar situations (Kendon and Ferber, 1973).

3.3 Robot gestures to express mental states

In the first two studies the robot used non-verbal behaviors that were modeled on human behavior. We now describe a pilot study, conducted in the wild, that moves toward metaphorical gestures. This study focused on gestures to express the following mental states of the robot: *agreement*, *disagreement*, *uncertainty*, and *excitement*. In humans, facial expressions and head gestures play an important role in expressing these mental states. While SARAH can produce different facial displays, she does not have a movable head. Based on our intuition, we devised the following non-verbal behaviors.

agreement Smile and move forward and backward a few inches.

disagreement Frown and rotate side to side by 35 degrees.

uncertainty With a neutral facial expression, turn away from the addressee by 45 degrees, briefly pause, then return.

excitement With surprised facial expression, spin around 360 degrees.

SARAH recruited subjects in a busy hallway on campus. She instructed subjects to retrieve an index card with a set of yes/no questions from a pocket attached to the robot and to ask those questions. SARAH accompanied her spoken answer either with facial expressions only or with facial expressions and gestures. At the end of the scripted interaction, SARAH said "Yay, we completed the task" and expressed excitement.

SARAH then asked the subjects to complete a paper survey rating SARAH's intelligence and naturalness. In this pilot study, SARAH's use of gestures did not have a (statistically significant) impact on people's perceptions of her. And, unfortunately, we did not collect data that allows us to draw conclusions on whether humans interpreted the gestures as intended.

Interesting research problems that arise are the design of easy to interpret metaphorical gestures, how to select which signals to use in a given dialog situation, how to coordinate different communicative signals, and how to transition between and blend different non-verbal behaviors.

Future work: We are preparing a follow up study that will evaluate the interpretability of variants of different gestures more systematically. Our goal is to create a lexicon of robot behaviors that can perform different discourse and dialog functions. We are currently focusing on robot movements, but we are also interested in other signals, like non-speech sounds and visual cues on the screen that go beyond facial expressions mimicking humans.

4 Conclusion

The interactions between humans and robots in public spaces are situated in an un-controllable and only partially predictable environment. This creates challenges for communication. We think that NLG can contribute to a solution to these challenges by producing utterances and other communicative behaviors that are adapted to the situation. In addition, we argue that these challenges give rise to research problems that are interesting from an NLG point of view.

In this paper, we have illustrated our position by describing three studies that explore the generation of co-verbal communicative behaviors for non-humanoid robots. This line of research tackles the following issues related to the generation of multimodal utterances. We need to design non-verbal signals that are mimicking human behavior as well as signals that communicate metaphorically. The robot behaviors are constrained by the limited motor capabilities of the robot, but they can also take advantage of expressive options that are not available to humans. We need techniques for generating multimodal utterances that coordinate the different non-verbal signals and speech. And finally, we need to understand how to choose the most effective set of signals in a given dialog situation.

References

James Allen, George Ferguson, and Amanda Stent. 2001. An architecture for more realistic conversational systems. In *Proc. of the 6th International Conference on Intelligent User Interfaces*.

Cynthia Lynn Breazeal. 2000. *Sociable machines: Expressive social exchange between humans and robots*. Ph.D. thesis, MIT.

Hendrik Buschmeier, Timo Baumann, Benjamin Dosch, Stefan Kopp, and David Schlangen. 2012. Combining incremental language generation and incremental speech synthesis for adaptive information presentation. In *Proc. of the 13th Annual Meeting of the Special Interest Group on Discourse and Dialogue*.

Aaron G. Cass, Eric Rose, Kristina Striegnitz, and Nick Webb. 2015. Determining appropriate first contact distance: trade-offs in human-robot interaction experiment design. In *Proc. of the Workshop on Designing and Evaluating Social Robots for Public Settings at the Intl. Conf. on Intelligent Robots and Systems*.

Aaron G. Cass, Kristina Striegnitz, Nick Webb, and Venus Yu. 2018. Exposing real-world challenges using HRI in the wild. In *Proc. of the 4th Workshop on Public Space Human-Robot Interaction at the Intl. Conf. on Human-Computer Interaction with Mobile Devices and Services*.

Justine Cassell, Joseph Sullivan, Elizabeth Churchill, and Scott Prevost. 2000. *Embodied Conversational Agents*. MIT press.

Elizabeth Cha, Yunkyung Kim, Terrence Fong, and Maja J. Matarić. 2018. A survey of nonverbal signaling methods for non-humanoid robots. *Foundations and Trends in Robotics*, 6(4):211–323.

Elizabeth Cha and Maja Matarić. 2016. Using nonverbal signals to request help during human-robot collaboration. In *Proc. of the Intl. Conf. on Intelligent Robots and Systems*.

Nicole Chovil. 1991. Discourse-oriented facial displays in conversation. *Research on Language and Social Interaction*, 25(1-4):163–194.

Herbert H. Clark and Meredyth A. Krych. 2004. Speaking while monitoring addressees for understanding. *J. of Memory and Language*, 50(1):62–81.

Anca D. Dragan, Kenton C.T. Lee, and Siddhartha S. Srinivasa. 2013. Legibility and predictability of robot motion. In *Proc. of the 8th Intl. Conf. on Human-Robot Interaction*.

Paul Ekman and Wallace V. Friesen. 2003. *Unmasking the Face: A Guide to Recognizing Emotions From Facial Expressions*. Malor Books.

Joy E. Hanna and Susan E. Brennan. 2007. Speakers' eye gaze disambiguates referring expressions early during face-to-face conversation. *J. of Memory and Language*, 57(4):596–615.

Dai Hasegawa, Justine Cassell, and Kenji Araki. 2010. The role of embodiment and perspective in direction-giving systems. In *Proc. of the AAAI fall symposium: Dialog with robots*.

Kristiina Jokinen and Graham Wilcock. 2003. Adaptivity and response generation in a spoken dialogue system. In Jan van Kuppevelt and Ronnie W. Smith, editors, *Current and new directions in discourse and dialogue*. Springer.

Adam Kendon. 1967. Some functions of gaze-direction in social interaction. *Acta Psychologica*, 26:22–63.

Adam Kendon and Andrew Ferber. 1973. A description of some human greetings. In *Comparative Ecology and Behaviour of Primates: Proc. of a Conf. held at the Zoological Society London*. Academic Press.

Alexander Koller, Kristina Striegnitz, Donna Byron, Justine Cassell, Robert Dale, Johanna Moore, and Jon Oberlander. 2010. The first challenge on generating instructions in virtual environments. In E. Krahmer and M. Theune, editors, *Empirical Methods in Natural Language Generation*, volume 5980 of *LNCS*. Springer.

David McNeill. 1992. *Hand and mind: What gestures reveal about thought*. University of Chicago Press.

Verena Rieser, Oliver Lemon, and Simon Keizer. 2014. Natural language generation as incremental planning under uncertainty: adaptive information presentation for statistical dialogue systems. *IEEE/ACM Transactions on Audio, Speech, and Language Processing*, 22(5).

Maha Salem, Stefan Kopp, Ipke Wachsmuth, Katharina Rohlfing, and Frank Joublin. 2012. Generation and evaluation of communicative robot gesture. *Intl. J. of Social Robotics*, 4(2):201–217.

Cameron Smith, Nigel Crook, Simon Dobnik, Daniel Charlton, Johan Boye, Stephen Pulman, Raul Santos De La Camara, Markku Turunen, David Benyon, Jay Bradley, et al. 2011. Interaction strategies for an affective conversational agent. *Presence: Teleoperators and Virtual Environments*, 20(5):395–411.

Marilyn A. Walker, Amanda Stent, François Mairesse, and Rashmi Prasad. 2007. Individual and domain adaptation in sentence planning for dialogue. *J. of Artificial Intelligence Research*, 30.

Being Data-Driven is Not Enough: Revisiting Interactive Instruction Giving as a Challenge for NLG

Sina Zarrieß and **David Schlangen**
Dialogue Systems Group // CITEC // Faculty of Linguistics and Literary Studies
Bielefeld University, Germany
{sina.zarriess,david.schlangen}@uni-bielefeld.de

Abstract

Modeling traditional NLG tasks with data-driven techniques has been a major focus of research in NLG in the past decade. We argue that existing modeling techniques are mostly tailored to textual data and are not sufficient to make NLG technology meet the requirements of agents which target fluid interaction and collaboration in the real world. We revisit interactive instruction giving as a challenge for data-driven NLG and, based on insights from previous GIVE challenges, propose that instruction giving should be addressed in a setting that involves visual grounding and spoken language. These basic design decisions will require NLG frameworks that are capable of monitoring their environment as well as timing and revising their verbal output. We believe that these are core capabilities for making NLG technology transferrable to interactive systems.

1 Introduction

The past decade has seen substantial progress in data-driven methods for natural language generation (NLG). It is now widely agreed that data-driven techniques are needed to obtain NLG systems that are adaptive and human-like (Belz, 2008), domain-independent (Wen et al., 2016), and – with recent methods from vision & language cf. (Bernardi et al., 2016) – suitable for agents that interact with humans in a physical environment (such as dialogue systems or robots) (Kazemzadeh et al., 2014). Despite this progress, however, data-driven NLG is rarely used in current real-world interactive systems, where more traditional (template-based) approaches for generating verbal output still persist.

In this paper, we argue that existing methods in data-driven modeling for NLG are heavily tailored to textual data and, therefore, fail to meet the requirements of dialogue systems, social agents or robots which target fluid interaction and collaboration in the real world. In the traditional view, the NLG task is usually framed as follows: given some non-verbal piece of data as input (e.g. sensor data, a meaning representation, facts from a knowledge base), the system needs to decide *what* to say (do content selection, text or sentence planning, micro-planning), and *how* to say it (do lexicalization, surface realization), cf. (Reiter and Dale, 1997). While recent data-driven systems have mostly overcome previous modular architectures that assigned these decisions to separate components in the processing pipeline (Konstas and Lapata, 2013), they still follow basic assumptions related to how the system processes its non-linguistic input and verbal output:

- static input: NLG systems are usually trained to map a given input to some written output, meaning that the environment does not change while the system is producing output
- perfect input: NLG systems are often trained on perfect representations of an environment or a knowledge base
- one-shot output: NLG systems do not need to monitor whether the listener has actually understood the output, strategies that are frequent in conversation (revision, correction, installments) do not have to be considered
- no temporal dimension: NLG systems assume that their output is not immediately consumed, i.e. it does not need to be packaged or timed (e.g. a text is produced as a whole)

Proceedings of the Workshop on NLG for Human–Robot Interaction, pages 27–31,
Tilburg, The Netherlands, November 8, 2018. © 2018 Association for Computational Linguistics

These assumptions are convenient when framing NLG tasks as machine learning problems (e.g. as ranking, classification or sequence-to-sequence learning), but they are highly problematic for interactive systems. To illustrate this point, we propose to revisit instruction giving as a challenge for data-driven NLG in interactive systems: here, a human instruction follower (IF) and an agent as the instruction giver (IG) have to achieve a common goal in a visual environment (e.g. find a route or treasure, assemble an object). The IG knows how to complete the task (e.g. where the treasure is, how the object looks like) but cannot affect the environment. The IF can affect the environment and the objects in it, but needs the IG's instructions to achieve the goal. In the context of the GIVE challenge (Byron et al., 2007), this setting has received considerable attention in the NLG community for some time (Byron et al., 2009; Striegnitz et al., 2011), but has not been developed further since then.

Generally, we believe that future approaches to instruction giving in NLG should extend GIVE along the following dimensions, in order to enable transfer of NLG technology to real-world applications like robots or dialogue systems:

- vision: generating instructions from a low-level visual representation of the environment, i.e. without perfect access to visually present objects and their properties
- spoken language: generating spoken instructions, such that the IF's non-verbal actions can happen concurrently with the IG's verbal utterances
- timing and information delivery: going beyond traditional NLG approaches focussing on content selection and/or surface realization, and move to real-time incremental processing that captures the affordances of spoken language and fluid interaction

In the following, we will show that these points constitute considerable challenges for the state-of-the-art in data driven NLG research and outline directions for how they could be addressed.

2 Visual grounding for instructions

A fundamental design decision in GIVE was to use a virtual environment such that the NLG systems had access to a perfect symbolic representation of

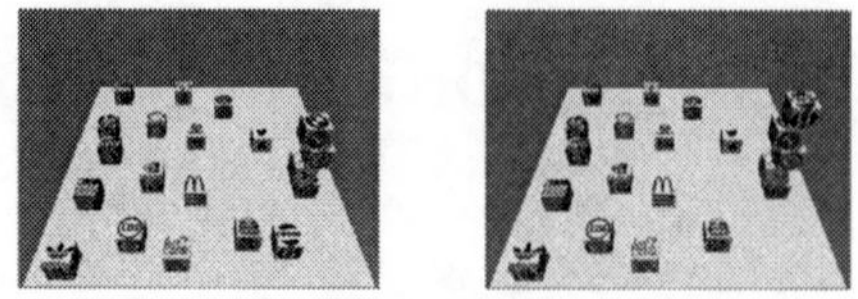

place the block that is to the right of the stella block as the highest block on the board. it should be in line with the bottom block .

Figure 1: Instruction example in the BLOCKS data set (Bisk et al., 2018)

the visually present objects and their properties. In the meantime, a lot of research in human-robot interaction has be done on modeling instructions in more realistic visual environments, though this community has often focussed on grounding verbal instructions to robot actions, cf. (Chai et al., 2018). Bisk et al. (2016) have proposed a nice formulation of a move-by-move instruction following task in an object assembly domain (see Figure 1): given an image of the current state of an environment (left image) and a verbal instruction, the task is to predict the target state of the environment after executing the instruction (right image). This move-by-move setting abstracts away from the internal action representations of a robot and also from general aspects of planning.

We believe that this set-up is promising for NLG as well, where the task would be to generate a verbal instruction that enables the IF to execute a particular action or achieve a state change of the environment, while the system (the IG) is given the current and the goal state of an environment as an image. This would be natural extension of existing language generation systems that are able to generate descriptions of real-world images (Bernardi et al., 2016), or referring expressions to objects in real-world images (Yu et al., 2017). At the same time, it would require systems to go beyond the commonly used CNN-LSTM architecture (Vinyals et al., 2015; Devlin et al., 2015; Mao et al., 2016; Yu et al., 2017) as these currently only map visual representations of single images or objects to verbal output. Instead, a visually grounded instruction generation system needs to reason about expressions that relate the current visual state to a target state, such as *place the block to the right (source state) as the highest block on the board (target state)* in Figure 1.

Conceptually, the problem of generating instructions in object assembly domains is similar to generating relational referring expressions which have been a notorious challenge for referring expression generation in general (Krahmer and Van Deemter, 2012). Relational expressions are also challenging for neural architectures (Hudson and Manning, 2018), and grounding (understanding) of relational referring expressions has been addressed in some recent work (Cirik et al., 2018; Hu et al., 2017) following the idea of modular networks based on syntactic structures (Andreas et al., 2016). However, none of these models is designed for generating relational structures in verbal expressions, such as instructions.

3 Spoken language dynamics

From research on situated spoken dialogue, it is well known that spoken and written language bear very different affordances. In spoken communication, listeners react, both non-verbally and verbally, to what speakers are saying, while they are saying it; and speakers adapt what they are saying, based on the reactions (or lack thereof) that they get, while they are speaking. The field of Conversation Analysis (see (Stivers and Sidnell, 2012) for a recent overview) and, taking up and further developing some of their ideas, the work of Herbert (Clark, 1996) has done much to shed light on the intricate strategies that interactants follow to co-construct dialogue in this way.

Figure 2 illustrates some prominent strategies that speakers use to achieve task success in spoken communication, with an instruction giving example taken from our PentoRef data (Zarrieß et al., 2016). Here, the IF has to assemble an object out of Pentomino pieces while the IG observes his actions over a camera feed. During a time span of approximately 30 seconds, the IG produces 18 short utterances in total that instruct the IF what to do next (e.g. *turn to the left*), confirm the IF's action (*exactly*), or repair what she is currently doing (*to the left, this is to the right*). Also, interestingly, the final step of the instruction (i.e. how to put the target piece to its target location, image 10-12 in Figure 2) is left underspecified by the IG as it is obvious to the IF how to complete the task. This level of coordination and adaptation between speakers and listeners is impossible in written communication where verbal and non-vernal actions cannot happen concurrently.

Unfortunately, most research on data-driven NLG still focusses entirely on written text or typed utterances, even in the domain of dialogue, as existing platforms and workflows for data collection are radically more efficient for text as compared to speech. Also the GIVE setting used typed communication. An interesting pilot study on a spoken version of the GIVE challenge was carried out by (Striegnitz et al., 2012) who found that interactions between participants were faster, more natural and rich of conversational phenomena (e.g. installments) that cannot be observed in text or typed chat. Another promising the direction here is the platform developed by (Manuvinakurike and DeVault, 2015), which extends the standard procedure for collecting chat interactions via crowdsourcing to spoken dialogue.

4 Monitoring, timing, revision

When facing uncertainty through visual grounding and dynamics through spoken language, NLG systems will need to address a range of decisions that, currently, completely fall out of the scope of research in this area. In the interactive world, NLG needs to monitor the listener's reaction in real-time and be able to quasi-continuously decide *when* to produce verbal output and *how* to potentially revise previous or future output. Thus, in order to generate fluid instructions as in the interaction shown in Figure 2, it is precisely the combination of *when* to speak and *what* to say that matters: an utterance that is appropriate at a particular point in time, might already be perceived as inappropriate or confusing shortly after.

To the best of our knowledge, aspects of monitoring and timing have not been addressed in data-driven NLG frameworks, though incremental processing has been shown to be highly effective in experimental or rule-based settings, cf. (Skantze and Hjalmarsson, 2013; Skantze et al., 2014; Buß and Schlangen, 2010). In the dialogue community, specific tasks that involve timing have been modelled in a data-driven way, such as barge-in detection (Selfridge et al., 2013), *end-of-utterance* detection (Raux and Eskenazi, 2012; Maier et al., 2017)), or *turn-taking* (Skantze, 2017) .

Even less work has been carried out on NLG systems that are able to produce revision, repair or correction utterances which can be essential to achieve task success, as shown in Figure 2. In (Zarrieß and Schlangen, 2016), we have explored an installment-based approach in a referring expression generation system for objects in real-world images, and found that even simple,

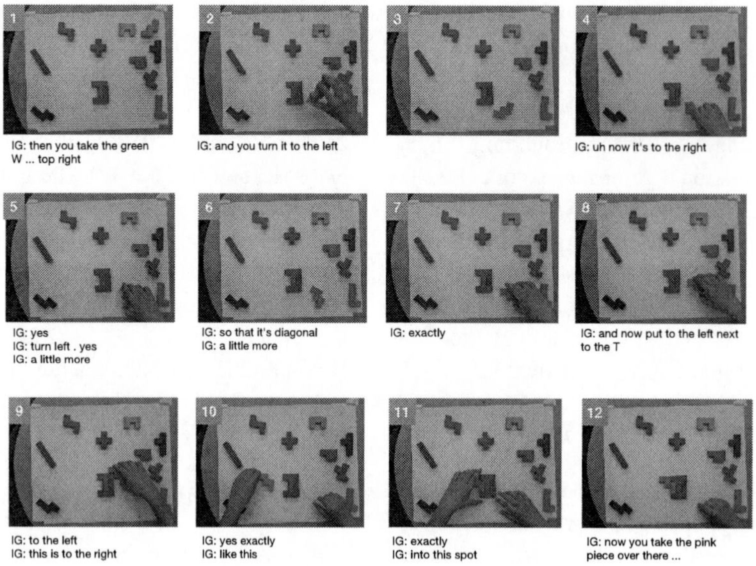

Figure 2: Example for task-oriented conversation in shared visual space from (Zarrieß et al., 2016): the joint task for the IF and IG is to build a puzzle out of Pentomino pieces where the IF can manipulate pieces on a physical gameboard and the IG sees the outline of the puzzle, observes the IF's actions in real-time (over a camera feed) and instructs the IF over headphones; the overall interaction time shown here is approx. 30 secconds; utterances have been translated to English from German transciptions

hand-crafted strategies for repair and revision very clearly improve the referential success of the system. (Villalba et al., 2017) propose a formal approach to generating contrastive referring expressions which is designed for similar scenarios. What is clearly missing to date, however, is a data-driven NLG framework that encompasses these various aspects of conversational grounding and timing in interaction.

5 Conclusion

This paper has discussed the task of interactive instruction giving from the perspective of data-driven NLG. We have argued that, if this task is set up so that it involves visual grounding and spoken language, it will constitute an interesting and considerable challenge for existing data-driven NLG frameworks. We believe that addressing this challenge and coming up with data collections and modeling methods for it will substantially forward the state-of-the-art in NLG, and foster transfer of NLG technology to real-world interactive systems.

References

Jacob Andreas, Marcus Rohrbach, Trevor Darrell, and Dan Klein. 2016. Neural module networks. In *Proceedings of the IEEE Conference on Computer Vision and Pattern Recognition*, pages 39–48.

Anja Belz. 2008. Automatic generation of weather forecast texts using comprehensive probabilistic generation-space models. *Natural Language Engineering*, 14(4):431455.

Raffaella Bernardi, Ruket Cakici, Desmond Elliott, Aykut Erdem, Erkut Erdem, Nazli Ikizler-Cinbis, Frank Keller, Adrian Muscat, and Barbara Plank. 2016. Automatic description generation from images: A survey of models, datasets, and evaluation measures. *J. Artif. Intell. Res.(JAIR)*, 55:409–442.

Yonatan Bisk, Kevin Shih, Yejin Choi, and Daniel Marcu. 2018. Learning interpretable spatial operations in a rich 3d blocks world. In *Proceedings of AAAI 2018*.

Yonatan Bisk, Deniz Yuret, and Daniel Marcu. 2016. Natural language communication with robots. In *Proceedings of the 2016 Conference of the North American Chapter of the Association for Computational Linguistics: Human Language Technologies*, pages 751–761.

Okko Buß and David Schlangen. 2010. Modelling sub-utterance phenomena in spoken dialogue systems. In *Proceedings of the 14th International Workshop on the Semantics and Pragmatics of Dialogue (Pozdial 2010)*, pages 33–41, Poznan, Poland.

Donna Byron, Alexander Koller, Jon Oberlander, Laura Stoia, and Kristina Striegnitz. 2007. Generating instructions in virtual environments (give): A challenge and an evaluation testbed for nlg. *Position Papers*, page 3.

Donna Byron, Alexander Koller, Kristina Striegnitz, Justine Cassell, Robert Dale, Johanna Moore, and Jon Oberlander.

2009. Report on the first nlg challenge on generating instructions in virtual environments (give). In *Proceedings of the 12th european workshop on natural language generation*, pages 165–173. Association for Computational Linguistics.

Joyce Y Chai, Qiaozi Gao, Lanbo She, Shaohua Yang, Sari Saba-Sadiya, and Guangyue Xu. 2018. Language to action: Towards interactive task learning with physical agents. In *IJCAI*, pages 2–9.

Volkan Cirik, Taylor Berg-Kirkpatrick, and Louis-Philippe Morency. 2018. Using syntax to ground referring expressions in natural images. *arXiv preprint arXiv:1805.10547*.

Herbert H. Clark. 1996. *Using Language*. Cambridge University Press, Cambridge.

Jacob Devlin, Hao Cheng, Hao Fang, Saurabh Gupta, Li Deng, Xiaodong He, Geoffrey Zweig, and Margaret Mitchell. 2015. Language models for image captioning: The quirks and what works. In *Proceedings of the 53rd Annual Meeting of the Association for Computational Linguistics and the 7th International Joint Conference on Natural Language Processing (Volume 2: Short Papers)*, pages 100–105, Beijing, China. Association for Computational Linguistics.

Ronghang Hu, Marcus Rohrbach, Jacob Andreas, Trevor Darrell, and Kate Saenko. 2017. Modeling relationships in referential expressions with compositional modular networks. In *Computer Vision and Pattern Recognition (CVPR), 2017 IEEE Conference on*, pages 4418–4427. IEEE.

Drew A Hudson and Christopher D Manning. 2018. Compositional attention networks for machine reasoning. *arXiv preprint arXiv:1803.03067*.

Sahar Kazemzadeh, Vicente Ordonez, Mark Matten, and Tamara L Berg. 2014. ReferItGame: Referring to Objects in Photographs of Natural Scenes. In *Proceedings of the Conference on Empirical Methods in Natural Language Processing (EMNLP 2014)*, pages 787–798, Doha, Qatar.

Ioannis Konstas and Mirella Lapata. 2013. A global model for concept-to-text generation. *J. Artif. Intell. Res.(JAIR)*, 48:305–346.

Emiel Krahmer and Kees Van Deemter. 2012. Computational generation of referring expressions: A survey. *Computational Linguistics*, 38(1):173–218.

Angelika Maier, Julian Hough, and David Schlangen. 2017. Towards deep end-of-turn prediction for situated spoken dialogue systems. In *Proceedings of Interspeech 2017*, Stockholm, Sweden.

Ramesh Manuvinakurike and David DeVault. 2015. Pair me up: A web framework for crowd-sourced spoken dialogue collection. In *Natural Language Dialog Systems and Intelligent Assistants*, pages 189–201. Springer.

Junhua Mao, Huang Jonathan, Alexander Toshev, Oana Camburu, Alan Yuille, and Kevin Murphy. 2016. Generation and comprehension of unambiguous object descriptions.

Antoine Raux and Maxine Eskenazi. 2012. Optimizing the turn-taking behavior of task-oriented spoken dialog systems. *ACM Transactions on Speech and Language Processing (TSLP)*, 9(1):1.

Ehud Reiter and Robert Dale. 1997. Building applied natural language generation systems. *Natural Language Engineering*, 3(1):57–87.

Ethan Selfridge, Iker Arizmendi, Peter Heeman, and Jason Williams. 2013. Continuously predicting and processing barge-in during a live spoken dialogue task. In *Proceedings of the SIGDIAL 2013 Conference*, pages 384–393.

Gabriel Skantze. 2017. Towards a general, continuous model of turn-taking in spoken dialogue using lstm recurrent neural networks. In *Proceedings of the 18th Annual SIGdial Meeting on Discourse and Dialogue*, pages 220–230.

Gabriel Skantze and Anna Hjalmarsson. 2013. Towards incremental speech generation in conversational systems. *Computer Speech & Language*, 27(1):243–262.

Gabriel Skantze, Anna Hjalmarsson, and Catharine Oertel. 2014. Turn-taking, feedback and joint attention in situated human–robot interaction. *Speech Communication*, 65:50–66.

Tanya Stivers and Jack Sidnell. 2012. Introduction. In Jack Sidnell and Tanya Stivers, editors, *The Handbook of Conversation Analysis*, chapter 1, pages 1–8. Wiley-Blackwell, Oxford, U.K.

Kristina Striegnitz, Hendrik Buschmeier, and Stefan Kopp. 2012. Referring in installments: a corpus study of spoken object references in an interactive virtual environment. In *Proceedings of the Seventh International Natural Language Generation Conference*, pages 12–16.

Kristina Striegnitz, Alexandre Denis, Andrew Gargett, Konstantina Garoufi, Alexander Koller, and Mariët Theune. 2011. Report on the second second challenge on generating instructions in virtual environments (give-2.5). In *Proceedings of the 13th European Workshop on Natural Language Generation*, pages 270–279.

Martin Villalba, Christoph Teichmann, and Alexander Koller. 2017. Generating contrastive referring expressions. In *Proceedings of the 55th Annual Meeting of the Association for Computational Linguistics (Volume 1: Long Papers)*, volume 1, pages 678–687.

Oriol Vinyals, Alexander Toshev, Samy Bengio, and Dumitru Erhan. 2015. Show and tell: A neural image caption generator. In *Computer Vision and Pattern Recognition*.

Tsung-Hsien Wen, Milica Gasic, Nikola Mrkšić, Lina M. Rojas Barahona, Pei-Hao Su, Stefan Ultes, David Vandyke, and Steve Young. 2016. Conditional generation and snapshot learning in neural dialogue systems. In *EMNLP*, pages 2153–2162, Austin, Texas. ACL.

Licheng Yu, Hao Tan, Mohit Bansal, and Tamara L Berg. 2017. A joint speaker-listener-reinforcer model for referring expressions. In *CVPR 2017*.

Sina Zarrieß, Julian Hough, Casey Kennington, Ramesh Manuvinakurike, David DeVault, Raquel Fernandez, and David Schlangen. 2016. Pentoref: A corpus of spoken references in task-oriented dialogues. In *10th edition of the Language Resources and Evaluation Conference*.

Sina Zarrieß and David Schlangen. 2016. Easy things first: Installments improve referring expression generation for objects in photographs. In *Proceedings of the 54th Annual Meeting of the Association for Computational Linguistics (Volume 1: Long Papers)*, pages 610–620, Berlin, Germany. Association for Computational Linguistics.

Author Index

André, Elisabeth, 12

Bateman, John, 17
Belakova, Jekaterina, 8

Cass, Aaron G., 22

de Haas, Mirjam, 1
de Wit, Jan, 1

Gkatzia, Dimitra, 8

Krahmer, Emiel, 1

Malaka, Rainer, 17

Pomarlan, Mihai, 17
Porzel, Robert, 17

Ritschel, Hannes, 12

Schlangen, David, 27
Striegnitz, Kristina, 22

Vogt, Paul, 1

Webb, Nick, 22
Willemsen, Bram, 1

Zarrieß, Sina, 27

Association for Computational Linguistics
209 N. Eighth Street
Stroudsburg, Pennsylvania 18360

ISBN 978-1-5108-7755-9

CURRAN ASSOCIATES INC.
proceedings.com